"Happily Ever After", It's Not Just for Fairy Tales

A guide from dating to retirement that will help you build a loving lifelong marriage.

By: Scott Averitt

Illustrations By: Heather Averitt, Samantha Averitt, & Isabella Averitt

I dedicate this book to my loving wife Heather and my two glorious daughters Samantha and Isabella.

They are not only the inspiration behind my life, but without them in my world, the words within this book would have no meaning.

Contents

Introduction

At 42 years of age I have realized that I have many responsibilities and diverse roles that fill my everyday life. Financial planner, employee, son, boss, friend, colleague, brother, handyman, mechanic, coach, computer guru, and the list goes on. But the most important responsibilities and roles a man can ever have is that of a husband and a father. I have been married to the love of my life for twenty-one glorious years and I am the proud father of two very intelligent, strong, beautiful daughters. I decided to write this book for one reason alone, I wanted to do everything I could to help my daughters find the same happiness and pure joy that their Mother and I share.

As I watch my daughters grow up, currently 15 and 18, to become young women I become increasingly more concerned with what their future holds for them. Have I been there when they needed me the most? Will they come to me when times get tough? Have I been the kind of father and husband that they will eventually strive to find as they go out into the world on their own? Even though I am now in my 40's I can remember myself during those impressionable young adult years. I was like every other teenager, I knew it all, and the last thing I wanted to hear was advice from some over the hill, outdated, out of touch, old person who didn't understand the world of today. This may sound familiar to those reading this who have gone through the teenage years with their own children. Don't get me wrong, my daughters are very mature and very respectful of me and their mother. Despite this I am also a realistic person and I know that if they are truly listening to half of what I say than I am doing pretty good. This is clear by the eye rolls and looks of discontent every time I start to "lecture" them on the ways of the force. For this reason, I thought it would be a good idea to write down all my ramblings so that perhaps later in life, when they didn't just look at my talks as a "lecture", they could take what advice would help them when they needed it the most.

I started writing down my thoughts and I quickly realized that my advice and insight was not only aimed at what would be applicable to my daughters, but it would also serve for their future boyfriends and eventually their husband. This is when I decided that this book could serve as a guide for both individuals and for couples. Let's face it, any team who wants to win the game better have a sound playbook that they can draw from. In fact, a team is exactly what a good marriage is all about. Even the great Michael Jordan needed the rest of his team to be successful himself.

I am the first person to admit that I do not have a doctorate in psychology, nor have I studied the so-called experts on marriage and children. The fact is that I have a Bachelor of Science in Electrical Engineering which probably makes me more qualified to fix your computer than your marriage. What I will tell you is that with the help of my wife I have learned what makes a marriage happy and successful. To be honest happy and successful is not strong enough to represent my relationship with my wife. My wife is my companion, my rock, my lover, my partner, and my best friend. She is there for me during the good times and the bad. She laughs at my stupid jokes. She corrects me when I screw up. She supports me through all that I do. She celebrates with me during the great times. She cries with me during the bad times. She lifts me up when I'm feeling down. She takes care of our daughters in a way I never could. She is my everything. This does not mean we have not had rough times. Marriage is hard work, but it can also be indescribably spectacular. Over the years my wife and I have found ourselves in a position where our friends have come to us for help with their relationships. We have not always been able to help them resolve their issues the way they would like, but it certainly has helped us to see areas where we could improve our relationship even further. At first this may seem rather callus and selfish of me but throughout the following chapters I will address the various reasons why things don't always work out the way we would like. Let's be honest, what we want is not always what is best for us or our spouse.

My wife and I have found things that work for us. This doesn't mean that all the ideas in this book will work for you. However, the fundamentals of marriage are the same, it is up to you and your spouse to find the particular things that work best for your relationship. I will cover the fundamentals of marriage later in this book.

Chapter 1

Ten signs your companion may not be "the one".

How do I know if he/she is "the one" for me? If you find yourself asking this question you may in fact need to answer another more important question first. Why am I asking if they are the one for me? Before you can determine if the person your dating is the person you will spend the rest of your life with, you first need to know what you want. A look into your desires and aspirations is very important. After all, if you don't know what you want how you can begin to ask the first question. One of the biggest mistakes you can make in marriage is to rush into it when you are not ready yourself. If you cannot honestly answer these next few questions with a resounding YES, then you probably need to spend more time on self-discovery before entering into marriage.

1. **Am I ready to give up all my free time for the sole purpose of making sure my spouse is happy?**

At first many people will read that question and cringe. "What do you mean I have to give up my free time just to make them happy, what about them making me happy?" Before you declare this book rubbish and get ready to torch it remember that marriage is a compromise. It also means that you make an oath to God and your spouse that you will be by their side in good times and bad. This does not mean that once you get married you will not have any time to yourself. This is quite the opposite as time to yourself is one of the foundations of a good marriage, I will talk more about this later. What this really means is that if you are not willing to give up your free time to do things for your spouse then you are either not ready for marriage or you have not found "the one". When my wife went through postpartum depression after the birth of our second daughter there was no question in my mind that I would be there by her side to help her through it. It also meant that I went from helping my wife with our oldest daughter to becoming the primary care giver for both my daughters and my wife. I thank God for the boundless help that we received from both of our families during this rough time. The point I am trying to make here is that in life unexpected things happen. Marriage means that you will stick by your spouse's side no matter what happens or for how long it endures. Therefore, it is so important for you to be able to answer this question with a resounding emphatic YES. One of the best parts of marriage is that I know no matter what life brings my wife will always be there by my side.

2. Am I willing to pool my financial resources with that of my spouse?

Now some of you might be saying "wait a second, I thought love would be at least #2 if it wasn't #1 on the list. After all money can't buy love or happiness, right?" Your right, or at least partially right. Money can't buy love, but it can pay for food, shelter, clothing, and a few other essential items needed to survive. Don't get me wrong, I'm a hopeless romantic and I strongly believe that if you have love than the rest doesn't matter. However, the truth is that you will find it very hard to love your spouse if they just spent all your food and rent money on the latest smart phone or a designer purse. Disagreements about finances is one of the largest sources of discourse within a marriage. Therefore, it is absolutely imperative to come to an agreement on how to handle things very soon after you have realized this person might be "the one".

I strongly recommend pooling your money to cut back on issues that will arise. One of the main reasons for this is that there is a good chance that one of you will make more money than the other. If you try to keep your finances separate there will inevitably be arguments about who pays for what. Perhaps you might be able to come to an agreement that seems to work but the risk is that there will always be one of you with some deep-down feeling that you are getting taken advantage of. Pooling your money together also means that you must agree as a couple on how to spend these finances. This does not mean that you need to ask each other before buying a cup of coffee, but the conversation should include if your spouse minds if you spend $6.95 twice a day on a grande mocha chino non-fat whatever. That's $417 a month for all of you out there trying to do the math in your head. Obviously, this is just one example and the amounts are all relative to what your total household finances are. Setting a weekly spending allowance for each of you is a very important part of making it work. This is also a great way to help the both of you to reach your financial and personal goals together. Finances are always changing so discussion and compromise must continue throughout the relationship. I should also caution you here to not pool your finances too early in a relationship before you are certain that you are heading down the path to marriage. This may seem a little like double speak where I am telling you to do one thing but then telling you to do the other. There is no one right answer as to when to start pooling your money. This will vary depending on the level of trust in your relationship. I can tell you that if you can't trust your significant other with your money than you are definitely not ready to be married to that person. My wife and I started pooling our money shortly after we agreed that we were going to get married. In our case this time came even before I proposed. Pooling our money early on helped us to save up for our rings and our wedding.

3. **Am I ready to share any secrets that I have with my spouse?**

Yes secrets, this includes past, present, and future. Remember what you're striving for in a relationship. You are looking for a spouse who will be by your side no matter what happens. This absolutely requires complete and unwavering trust with your spouse. If you can't trust your significant other than stop reading this book now and figure out a way to earn each other's trust before you do another thing. All relationships are built on trust. This is true for your friends, colleagues, employees, children, and most importantly your spouse. I know that sometimes the truth may seem harder than keeping the secret but, trust me, your relationship will be much stronger without any secrets. Now I am not suggesting that you start airing all your dirty laundry on the first date. That is unless you want to spend the rest of your life alone. If you have a secret that you are ready to share, make sure you find the appropriate time and sit down to discuss this with your significant other. Blurting out that you have six toes while sitting down for a romantic dinner may not be a smart thing to do, great conversation starter but it can come off a bit creepy. Getting back to seriousness now, plan to talk with them in a private setting when you have plenty of time to discuss things afterwards. Keep in mind that secrets don't always have to be bad things. Some secrets are about your dreams and aspirations in life.

4. **Do I think about him/her when we are apart?**

I have been with my wife for over 20 years and I can honestly say that there is not a day when we are apart where I am not thinking about her throughout the day. I will admit that it is not every second of every day, let's be realistic. But when I am at work or especially when I am away on a business trip I do find myself wishing that I was by her side or wondering how her day is going. I don't want to scare you at this point and cause you to wonder, "do I think about him/her often enough? Am I really in love? Oh no what am I doing wrong?". There is no right or wrong regarding how many times you think about him/her. What matters here is that you do think about them when you are not together. If you can go 2 or 3 days without some sort of communication or contact and they never cross your mind even once then you might need to ask yourself if this is really the right person for me. Please don't take this as a way to test their love for you by not talking to them until they talk to you first. All this will do is tear you up inside and you will ultimately develop harsh feelings for the other person. After all, "I have been thinking about them all day and they have not even texted me once." This is not about them but rather about you. I will further caution you that this is by no means a green light for you to text and call them every 10 minutes. That may be great if both of you are having fun with it, but it can quickly turn into the perception of stalking and obsession.

With technology these days there are so many ways to let your loved one know you're thinking about them. My wife and I used to send love messages via pagers when we first started dating. For the younger crowd reading this, a pager was like a text message but only with numbers. I get it, I am getting old, now moving on. My point is that with these gadgets at your fingertips you should be using them to your advantage to let your loved one know you care and that you're thinking about them. When I am having a rough day, nothing cheers me up more than seeing a text from my wife simply stating, "I love you" followed by a clever emoji. If you don't know what a text message is then it's probably too late for you, stick to pen and paper.

Technology is not the only way to show your loved one you care. Notes on their windshield, flowers for no reason, sticky notes on the bathroom mirror, among many other possibilities are all great ways to build your relationship even further. In a later chapter, I will cover countless ideas that can be used to express your love that should be used often throughout your marriage.

5. Is he/she my best friend?

This one is more important than you may think. Physical Attraction to your significant other is extremely important but it is not everything. In fact, attraction can be broken into at least two different types, physical and physiological. Everybody understands physical attraction and it is the one thing that most likely grabbed your attention when you first met. Although physical attraction is important it also is the one that will most likely change throughout your relationship. I don't care who you are, but it is impossible to be sexy when your hunched over the toilet with the stomach flu. That's obviously one less than pleasant example but my point is that physical attraction is not what makes for long lasting relationships. It is what gives you the butterflies in your stomach when you see the other person, but this does not last forever, and it certainly is not the definition of love.

On the other hand, physiological attraction is what you find appealing about the other person's character and personality. These are the things that make you laugh, smile, and well, feel comfortable. Think of how your best friend has made you feel through the years of school and even afterwards. These are the feelings that stay with you as a couple for a lifetime. Some of the best relationships are where two people started out as friends and then became a couple later on. This is one of the many reasons why sex can wait till after you're married. As my daughters tell me every time, here comes the lecture. Don't worry, I am not going to get all religious on you here. Not to say that God isn't the most important part of any relationship but there is another best seller out there on that subject, and frankly the authors of that book are way out of my league. Anyway, sex has a way of complicating a relationship if the other foundational values are not well established first. To be very direct, if your significant other can't wait till you're ready to have sex than this should be a red flag that they will run away at the first sign of trouble.

Best friends are the people that stick around even when you may not be the most pleasant to be around. This is a quality you absolutely want and should desire to have in a significant other. I know it may not seem sexy or alluring but bear with me for a minute. Life is full of good times and not so good times. It is the rough times in your life that will be the most trying on you and your marriage. These happen to also be the times when you need your spouse the most. Every one of us wants to have the person we love standing by our bed side when we're sick or when we need a warm embrace after receiving bad news. Although these times are tough they are not the roughest. At three o'clock in the morning and you're first born has been crying non-stop for 6hrs, you will be at your wits end, this is when you need your spouse. To avoid getting to dark and depressing I will spare you the hundreds of other life changing trials and tribulations that a person can face in their lifetime. Just think of your worst fear and then double it. Now think to yourself how important it would be to have your best friend, your spouse, right by your side the entire time. At this point you're probably saying "enough already... I get it, but how do I know if my significant other is truly my best friend and will stick by my side as you have said." Unfortunately, there are no magic words or neon signs that point this out. However, there are certainly many indicators in your relationship that can help you to determine this. I have talked to many people who have gone through a bad breakup or a divorce and many times I have heard them say "I should have known this was coming, the signs were all right in front of me." It is always easy to say things like that after the fact, but it is also a very true statement. Too often in relationships we are too much "in love" to notice the signs staring us in the face. You may even be kicking yourself saying "if I had just listened to my parents or my best friend or whomever".

A lot of what I am trying to say here goes back to the first 5 points, selfishness, communication, trust, companionship, and friendship. In fact, as the title of this chapter promised, the other 5 signs that indicate he/she is not the one takes the same 5 points and directs them at your significant other rather than yourself. If you can honestly say that your significant other scores high in all five of these categories than congratulations, it's time to go ring shopping. But if you take a closer look at these things and realize there are some issues than it's time to sit down with him/her and have some serious conversations about what is lacking. I do want to pause here a moment and say that you should not be looking for issues or overthinking things too much. The kind of indicators I am talking about are not subtle. They sometimes just get overlooked because we are too blinded by other things or because we don't want to admit something is wrong. What you need to pay attention to is recurring events or issues rather than a single occurrence. Just to make my point a little clearer I put together a list of things that should trigger you to think about your relationship in a different light.

- "I can't believe he/she said that to me, that is so mean."

- "I don't feel like he/she ever listens to me."

- "Why do we always have to do what he/she wants to do?"

- "he/she chose to go out drinking with his/her friends instead of going to my family's house for dinner."

- "I feel stupid around his/her friends, they make me feel inadequate."

- "When we're in a group with his/her friends I feel left out and ignored."

- "Why do I always have to be the responsible one?"

- "He/She always promises me this is the last time and it never is."

If any of these statements or something similar sounds familiar to you then you need to have a serious conversation with your significant other. Keep in mind the most important key word in that last sentence, "conversation". If the two of you cannot talk about these things now, like mature adults, without arguing than you have real issues that need to be addressed. It is entirely possible that your significant other is completely unaware of how you feel regarding these things. Having the conversation gives him/her the chance to make things right and to help resolve things before things get worse.

You also need to realize that some of these feelings may also be due to your own insecurities and have little to do with how your significant other is behaving. Without getting to far off subject I want to quickly mention one very important point relating to this. Part of a good marriage is knowing each other's insecurities and weaknesses. There are two main reasons why this is important. As a spouse, it is your responsibility to help your spouse with their insecurities and weaknesses. Not by lecturing them or by telling them to just get over it. It is your responsibility to shelter and protect them when they need you to and to support and encourage them to overcome their insecurities and weaknesses when they are ready. Secondly and most importantly, it is also your responsibility to never, I mean never, to use those insecurities and weaknesses against your spouse under any circumstance. A good marriage is based on trust and this is one of the fundamentals I will touch more on that later.

There are a couple of things that should never be overlooked and should be a clear indication that you need to end the relationship now. There simply is no excuse for physical or verbal abuse on behalf of either person. If you ever find yourself in a relationship where the other person strikes you or verbally berates you, end it now before it's too late. People that resort to this behavior need serious help and despite your best intentions you are not the one to help them get past it. Relationships that start this way almost never get better and, even if they don't end in tragedy, it is no way to live your life. It is most certainly NOT the environment in which to raise children. If I can make this clear to even one person who can then escape their torture than this entire book will be worth its existence. I plead with those of you reading this who endure this abuse at the hope they will change. Stop making excuses for their inexcusable behavior and run. There are many resources available that can help you and your children to escape this life and start new. I have listed a few of those resources in the appendix of this book but many others exist including your local church or your pastor.

Before I met my wife, I found myself often perplexed by many of the relationships around me. I noticed that in many cases guys who treated women poorly were often sought after by women the most. I never fully understood this dichotomy until after my wife and I had been together a while and we started to discuss this at length. We came to the not so surprising conclusion that women often find bad boys exciting. As we observed more of our friends and the relationships around us we noticed that this worked both ways. Guys also found women exciting that had a bit of a wild or unpredictable side. My wife admitted to me that at first, she was not particularly interested in me because I wasn't the kind of guy she was typically interested in. Let's face it, I'm an engineer and engineers are not exactly known for their wild and crazy personalities. Some people might say that we're even kind of boring...and for the most part we are...at least to non-engineers. With this realization, I finally understood some of the more peculiar things that were said to me by the opposite sex all those years ago. On more than one occasion I was told by women that "I was too nice to go out with". What does that even mean? I just figured this was their way of nicely telling me to "get lost weirdo". I now realize what they were getting at. I wasn't exciting, I wasn't a bad boy. Now before all you guys start thinking I just handed over the key to being a player, pay very close attention to the next statement.

"Bad boys are exciting ... especially when your waiting for their child support check!"

You heard me right. Bad boys are just that...boys. Last time I checked marriage was between a man and a woman not between a boy and a woman. This same phrase can be reversed to a man and a girl. The real point here is that although a "bad boy" or "bad girl" can be exciting at the beginning of a relationship, eventually one of you will grow up and realize what you really want is a spouse that is loving, caring, thoughtful, and giving.

Be careful that you're not marrying an immature person as this will most likely come back to haunt you. The good news is that immaturity is relatively simple to spot and a good indication that the person is not ready for the commitment of marriage. In fact, the five signs I already covered in this chapter are some of the best indicators. I must provide a word of caution and say that it is very important to note that maturity is not necessarily linked to someone's age as many people believe. I know many 17 and 18-year old's that are by far more mature than some 30 and even 40-year old's. I was 20 when I married my beautiful wife who had just turned 18 a few months prior. Don't get me wrong, we were both inexperienced and we a great deal of learning ahead of us, but neither of us were immature. There is no single action or event that determines a person's maturity. It is a culmination of many attributes that signify when a person is mature enough to enter into marriage. Being mature does not mean that you are no longer a fun person. Maturity is knowing the right moments in life when it's appropriate to laugh at your friend's unfortunate embarrassing moment and when you need to stand up in defense of that same friend. Maturity is about putting your loved ones needs ahead of yours. It's about taking responsibility for your actions and saying you're sorry when you screw up. It's about being respectful to others even when their being disrespectful and immature. Maturity is about making plans and taking action to ensure the safety and security of yourself and your family. Having a baby does not automatically make you mature. This should be clearly evident to anyone who has ever watched the TV show 16 and Pregnant.

Too many people in this world are quick to judge or label people based only on what they see on the surface. This was so abundantly clear to my wife and I when we would tell someone that we were getting married. More often than not, their next statement was "when is the baby due" or "your too young to get married". I have absolutely no regrets for getting married when we did, and I would do it all again just the same if I was given the chance. It is absolutely imperative that you and your girlfriend/boyfriend make the decision to get married based solely on your own decision. This does not mean however that you should completely ignore the opinions of your family and friends. Both of you need to listen to the opinions of your loved ones and ensure that you are truly prepared. Earlier in this chapter I talked about the regret that comes at the end of a messy breakup, especially when you were warned by someone who cares for you. A mature couple that is ready for marriage can sit down with one another and discuss the concerns from each other's family and friends. This will help to strengthen the relationship even further. It may be difficult for either of you to hear the concerns from the other's family and friends. After all, if you need to have a discussion regarding the comments then it's probably not regarding how wonderful a person they think he/she is. It is very important for both of you to remember that these comments are coming from family and friends who do not want to see their loved ones hurt. Don't take negative comments personally as they are generally more concerned with their loved one's wellbeing rather than concerning themselves with hurting your feelings. If you don't believe me now, you will when you have your own children and you are put in the same position.

I will also warn you that in some cases the comments and reservations you will get are at least in part due to your family having a difficult time of letting you go. This is not fair and it can make it very difficult for you to sort through. You will need to discern what parts are for your wellbeing and what is selfishness on behalf of your family. However, don't automatically dismiss comments from your family as selfishness. If you suspect this is happening, then strongly consider having a heart to heart with your family regarding this. Be careful here as they may not recognize this is happening themselves or they may be unwilling to admit it. It took me many years after my wife and I were married to recognize what was happening with my family at the time and it took even longer for me to forgive and forget as it was very hurtful to both of us. I had to discover this for myself as no one explained it to me back then. I hope that having gone through this trial will help me to curb my selfishness when my daughters are about to leave home and get married but I can't promise anything. Just a bit of a warning to any prospective future suitors out there, I may not have a gun, but I do have a black belt in Martial arts.

"We've been together forever but I'm just not sure… Blah blah blah..". I've heard this phrase more than once and to be honest I cringe every time. The length of time that you have been together is not irrelevant, but it certainly is less important than being able to seriously take an honest look at the topics in this chapter and to feel comfortable with what you discover. Just because you have been together long enough to qualify for common law marriage does not mean you will do well as a married couple. In fact, this can be quite the opposite. Odds are, the reason that the two of you are now talking about marriage is because one of you wants something else from the relationship. Perhaps it's true commitment, children, or simply being able to call your significant other your husband or wife. It's not always the case but chances are that one of you has been just fine with the relationship the way it is. That person doesn't really want anything to change. This is where you can get in trouble because that person may agree to marriage merely because they see it as way to keep the other person happy. They may be more interested in trying to keep things the way they are instead of progressing the relationship. In reality, the person who really wanted to get married may mistakenly take this as a sign that the other person wants the same things in life. This doesn't mean that things must change after you get married but to be brutally honest things will change. For myself and many others it changes for the better, but things definitely change. Don't fool yourself by thinking that you will stay the same person that you were in your twenties as you get into your thirties, forties, fifties… One of the most important parts of marriage is planning for the future. If your significant other doesn't want to plan your future together than this should be a good sign that they are not ready for marriage. It may be that you're the one who doesn't want things to change and essentially there is nothing wrong with this. You just need to be honest with your significant other and yourself. Although I say things change after you get married it's not like turning on a light switch. The change is generally more gradual as the two of you plan and live out your life together. The important thing to take away from this is that both of you need to understand that you will be entering a new phase of your life. Both of you need to approach this together and you need to collectively agree on how things will proceed. The next chapter will discuss the "must have" conversations before saying "I do". These topics should certainly be part of the discussions.

Before leaving this chapter, I want to touch on a very important concept that will help you seriously contemplate all the topics covered thus far.

People can change but only if they want to.

At first this may not seem like such a profound statement but let me explain why this is so important. As we have progressed through this chapter we have touched on many different topics which may have raised some red flags. When we are in love it is easy for us to overlook these red flags and play them off as not that important or that they don't matter. For some of the red flags this is probably the case and it may just be you over analyzing the situation. However, other red flags that you currently overlook for the sake of the relationship can balloon into major problems later down the road.

I want to pause for a brief moment and tell you that you will never find a mate where there is not at least one thing you would like them to change about themselves. You will most likely find multiple things about the other person that annoy you or drive you crazy in some way or another. The good news is that the same is true for them. There are things that you do that drive them mad even if they have never said a word about it. Now that I have stated the obvious and annoyed you for wasting your time, I will get to my point.

If you enter a relationship thinking that you can change the other person than you are most definitely wrong, and you could be setting yourself up for terrible hardship. I'm not saying that people can't change, I'm just saying that you can't make them change if they don't want to. It is a terrible mistake to dismiss something about your significant other's personality or habits that really bothers you while hoping that you can change them. People must want to change for it to happen. I am a firm believer of the following principals.

People can change but only if both of the following are true.
1. **The person must truly want to change.**
2. **The person is provided with the opportunity to change.**

The first principle is straightforward. For example, an alcoholic who wants to dry up has a good chance of success. On the other hand, an alcoholic who attends AA meetings just to get their family off their back is almost doomed to never kick the habit. Think of the age old saying, "you can bring a horse to water, but you can't make him drink." If a person recognizes what they are doing is bad for them or the relationship they have to make a choice. They can decide to continue as is or they can decide to correct that behavior. Only if they decide to make a change can things begin to head in the right direction.

The second principal is a bit more cryptic regarding the point I am trying to make. The best way to describe this is to start out with the following example. A 10-year old boy who wants to learn how to play baseball was given a bat, a glove, and a ball from his parents. However, despite many requests to his parents to go outside and play with him, he is met with lame excuses and disappointment. At first you might think that the child had the opportunity to learn because he was given the equipment he needed to learn. To some extent you would be right, after all the child has the opportunity to play with his friends. This is very true but what the boy really wanted was the chance to spend more time with his parents. I am not trying to turn this into a sob story but rather show that **opportunity** is more than just having the right **tools** at hand. Going back to the alcoholic example, you might say that everyone has the opportunity to get help because anybody can attend AA meetings. Again, this is true but what both examples are missing is the emotional support from someone who truly cares for their wellbeing. When I refer to **opportunity** I am speaking of both the necessary **tools** and the underlying **emotional** support and care that backs the person up.

To put this back into the context of a relationship I can think of many examples of where my wife has helped me to become a better person. She helped me to curb my swearing by gently reminding me when a choice word would slip out without me even really noticing. She has helped me to be a better father by encouraging me to get more involved with my daughter's lives. My wife has also been indescribably patient and supportive of helping me to become less dense when it comes to picking up on her subtle hints and clues when in public settings. These examples are cases where I either wanted to make improvements or where my wife wanted me to change my behavior to better our relationship and our family. Despite my desire to improve in these areas I would not have made much progress without her loving support. Please note that I said, "loving support". This is very different than badgering, nagging, or yelling. The latter terms are counterproductive to support your cause. The good thing about **loving support** is that it can often lead to encouraging your significant other to develop the desire to change for the sake of the relationship.

All the above is only possible with open communication. It is not a good idea to try and get these results through manipulation or guilt. Although these methods may have some results they will generally only be short lived and will often be met with significant resistance and discontent. It is also important to make sure that you're asking the person to change something that is truly for the benefit of the relationship or your family and not just for your benefit. The latter is selfish behavior and eventually it will most likely backfire on you. Alternatively, encouraging your significant other to better understand you and your desires is not selfish. Rather it is a conscious action that will truly better the relationship between the two of you. Also remember what I said earlier about the fact there are most likely some things your significant other would like to change about you. This is a two-way street, don't expect your significant other to make progress on the things you want if you are unwilling to reciprocate.

Chapter 2

Must have conversations before saying I do.

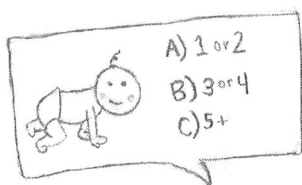

Congratulations...if your reading this you have passed the first set of hurdles from chapter 1 and you are moving on to the next challenge. The topics in this chapter will help you to have some serious conversations about your future life together. These discussions should go much smoother if the points from chapter 1 have been addressed or at the very least the two of you are working towards a resolution on these issues. It is also possible that some of these topics may actually spur further friction or bring new complications to the surface. Either way it is very important to truly understand your significant other's feelings on these matters. Waiting until after your engaged or worse yet, married, is a big mistake. Many of these topics can be a deal breaker or lead to turmoil in your marriage if the two of you cannot come to a common agreement.

Kids

At first the topic of children may seem very straight forward, after all it's a simple "yes or no". This is very true and if one of you absolutely wants to have children while the other person is firmly against it than you have a serious problem. The desire to have children or not is one that often cannot be swayed. This is very important as you may think the other person has finally caved on your pleas for children only to find that they will walk out on you and the children a few years down the road. First, I must say that leaving your spouse and children behind is the most cowardly and selfish act of betrayal that someone can do. Although this may be the worst-case scenario it is not the only unpleasant outcome. Arguments, lack of assistance raising the children, discontent, bitterness, resentment, and little to no involvement in their child's life are just a few of the damaging possibilities. I cannot stress enough how critical it is to be absolutely certain that both of you are completely forthright and honest regarding your answer. Children have the single largest impact on your life from conception till the day they stick you in a nursing home. A little side note to my daughters, you're not getting rid of your mother or I that easy so don't get any ideas. I am mostly kidding as ~~I know~~... I mean, ~~I hope~~ ... I pray they would take care of us as long as they could. Lol.

Simply agreeing that both of you want children should not be the end of the conversation. The next big question should be how many children you want. You don't necessarily need to agree on an exact number as that choice is not always up to the two of you. But you should agree if you want between one to three children or if you plan to have enough to fill out your own soccer team. Having seven kids is a lot different than two and both scenarios will affect planning of your future together in very different ways.

Equally important to the number of children is when you plan to have them. There are many factors that may influence someone's desire of when to have children. Financial security, college degree, career, and the size of your home are just a few of the logical reasonings that may impact your timing. Other considerations are more emotional and/or physiological than the prior list. Some people have grown up their entire life with the absolute desire to become a parent while others may feel they are too young or are getting too old to wait. There is no one size fits all regarding the importance or ranking of any of these reasons. Each person will have their own list with some variation as to their own priorities. In most cases this list and priorities will likely change many times as both of you get older and situations change. The most important thing to take away from this is that no single answer is the right answer. What is critical is that the two of talk about all these things and then work to find a common agreement that makes both of you happy. Keep in mind that a disagreement on whether to have children or not can be just as damaging to a relationship as fundamentally disagreeing on the timing or the number of children. It is also noteworthy that all the planning in the world may not matter as God may trump any decision the two of you come up with anyway. Triplets or an unplanned pregnancy can derail the best laid plans in a hurry.

Everyone is entitled to their own reasons for when they would like to start a family but, I would like to offer a few suggestions to discuss.

For most people, you will never be financially ready for children.

What I mean by this is that the two of you should be cautious of putting off having children until "things get better financially". This doesn't mean that you should start a family if you can't afford to feed the two of you or if your struggling to keep a roof over your head. Adding a child to that type of situation will most certainly make things more challenging. What I mean is that you should not set arbitrary financial goals as a precursor to having children. Statements like "When we make x amount of money" or "when I get my promotion" are usually non-deterministic and subject to change once you reach that goal. Waiting till you have a job that can support a family, having insurance to help pay for medical costs, or having a place to call your own where there is enough room to start a family are different and more realistic goals. These later goals are not essential towards having a child, but they will make the whole experience much more pleasant.

**Wait a few years after getting married
before having your first child.**

Take the first few years to get used to your new life together as a married couple. Get to know one another on a deeper level. Work through any issues that may still be lingering around. Enjoy the companionship of your spouse while you have undivided one on one time. After you have children the day to day dealings of running a household can add unwanted pressure on the marriage, especially if there is not a good foundation to build on. I will come back to this topic later, but it is worthwhile mentioning the importance of this while we're on the topic of planning and timing for children.

**If you're planning on going to college
full time I strongly recommend
waiting to have children until after
you graduate with your degree.**

The workload of a being a full-time college student is daunting. The challenge of performing well at work to support yourself and your wife while attending college full time is downright crazy. Trust me I can speak from experience on this one. But balancing a full-time career, 12-14 college credits, and a baby is absolutely insane!!!! If you can plan on not becoming parents until after one or both of you have your degree(s) your stress levels will be greatly reduced. I am not saying it's impossible to be married with kids while working full time and going to college, but the odds are that at least one of these things will suffer. The last thing you want to have happen is to look back when your kids are all grown up and wish you had spent more time with them when they were young.

Now that we have handled the topics of **if**, **when**, and **how many**, it's time to spend some time discussing how each of you see raising your children. Before you get too excited this book is not a "how to" manual for raising children. 18 years in and my wife and I are still learning and making mistakes as we go. But it is important to have an agreement on some of the basics very early on regarding your approach to raising children. For instance, public or private school, spankings or timeout, daycare or stay at home Mom or Dad? I obviously have my own strong opinions on these topics, as if you by now haven't figured out that I have an opinion on almost everything. I will get into the details of these later in the chapter on what to do with that little bundle of ... "Oh my... what did we get ourselves into". Just kidding, I wanted to make sure you were still paying attention. The idea here is once again, about communication and starting the dialog so that nobody is shocked later in life when one of you takes a stand on a particular topic. Unfortunately, you can't predict all scenarios because the world is ever changing. Communication remains key in all areas of your relationship.

Money

Ahh yes... we are back on that subject. In the first chapter we talked about pooling your finances together and coming to an agreement regarding how that money is spent. I believe that complete honesty and transparency regarding your finances is the only way to have a truly deep and loving relationship. I have seen many cases where couples use money as a weapon against each other. "Well he did this and spent this much so I am going to do what I want and spend the same". I can't even begin to put into words how destructive this mentality is to both your relationship and to your individual lives. There are no winners with this way of thinking. Not only is this behavior damaging it is also an indication of selfishness and immaturity.

Once you have established an agreement on how the finances will be handled it is also important to determine which one of you is going to take the lead. Despite the fact that the two of you need to collaborate on what to do with the money it is also a fact that you can't have two people driving the bus. Nothing will screw up your finances faster than thinking the other person paid the house payment when in reality the mortgage company is feeling a bit neglected. As an engineer I use a highly sophisticated spreadsheet that prevents me from ever making any errors…. I almost made it through that sentence without snickering. I am not sure that a full proof method exists for not making the occasional error and for this reason it is important to make sure there is some cash buffer in your bank account to cushion the blow of an unexpected bill or a slip up in accounting. It is also important to offer support to the person who takes the lead and remember they are human. So be forgiving if they make the occasional error or misstep. If they are stumbling like a newborn deer on a patch of ice it might be time for the two of you to agree on a new driver of the bus. Either way, make sure that your both on the same bus and that you agree on which direction the bus is going. Don't forget to agree on the driver or your finances are destined for the ditch on the side of the road.

Home is Where?

Do you have a dream of living in a particular city, state, country, or are you content wherever as long as it's close to family? If you have a preference than this should be discussed with your significant other before saying, "I do". It may not always be possible to live in your dream destination due to work, family, or finances but the two of you should at least be aware of each other's aspirations. As your life progresses together, circumstances will change and that may affect where you call home. If your spouse has always wanted to move out west but you absolutely don't want to move far away from your family, this can become a problem. Later in this book I will talk a little more about the important role that family plays in raising your children. Once again, a major disagreement on a topic like this can cause significant issues including separation and/or divorce. Communication and compromise will always be the key to avoiding major problems.

Sometimes moving is necessary to get or keep a job. Moving may also be necessary to further one of your careers or to follow a major opportunity that is their dream job. At the core of what I am trying to get at is that it is imperative to truly understand the deep desires of your significant other. If you can't live with the reality of those desires, you might want to rethink your relationship before you get married. I want to be explicitly clear on this subject. When I say someone has a deep desire to do something this should not be confused with a feeling of "it would be nice if one day I could ...". The best way to get my point across is probably with an example or two. A person who is driven to one day be an astronaut so much that they will stop at nothing to get there is completely different than someone who says it would be really cool to go for a ride on a spacecraft. A person with the aspirations and the means to become president of the United States will most likely not accept your desire to not move away from your parents when the opportunity arises to further their chances. These may be extreme examples but the same can be said for professionals that are set on furthering their career to ever increasing levels. If this does not bother you than that is great, and you should support them every step of the way.

God

Before I catch grief from everybody on why I placed this topic where I did. These topics are not placed in order of importance or in the exact order in which they should be discussed. If that were the case than God should be at the front of every paragraph in this book as God should always come first in your life and especially in your marriage. The fact is that not everyone is in the same place in their walk with the Lord. At the first mention of God some people would have put this book down rather than reading on. For this reason, I purposely chose to bring God into the discussion at this point.

With that being said, I have to touch on the topic of religious belief. Ideally everyone in the world would be at one with God and this would not be a subject that needed to be discussed prior to marriage. Unfortunately, this is not the case and it is critical that God is a big part of your relationship together. I think it goes without saying that you should not be entering into a relationship with someone who does not believe in God or Jesus Christ as their Savior. This is not to say that we should not be associating with people who do not believe in God. The truth is that Jesus spent much of his time on this Earth with non-believers. After all, how else can Christians spread the word of God if they don't interact with those who have not yet found their Savior. However, entering into a serious relationship with someone who does not share your hopes, dreams, morals, and beliefs will often place significant stress on the relationship. This doesn't mean that your significant other has to be in the same place as you are with God, but they should at least believe in God and have a desire to improve their relationship with him.

I would also like to be able to say that all Christian denominations are the same. I am not here to say that one denomination is better than the others, but I will tell you that there can be significant differences between them. Many of these variations have more to do with tradition rather than biblical principles but regardless they can quickly become a point of contention between the two of you if this has not been discussed at length. If the two of you come from different denominations, you will need to discuss which denomination that the two of you will choose going forward. You may even decide upon a different denomination all together, but you need to agree on one that both of you are comfortable with. Keep in mind that switching denominations may not go over so smoothly with either one of your families. Despite this, the decision is ultimately up to the two of you and the rest of your families will eventually be okay with it if you're making a Godly decision that is right for the two of you and your future children. Even more importantly it comes down to the relationship that the two of you have with God rather than the religious denomination.

In-laws

You can pick your friends, you can pick your spouse, you can even pick your nose, but you can't pick your family. This may sound bad at first, but truthfully it is rare that you will see eye to eye with your parents let alone your significant other's parents. Before you get too excited, getting married is not an excuse to cut ties and rebel against your family. Families can be difficult at times but in most cases, they are also the ones that will be there for you regardless of what happens. Obviously, this is not the case for everyone and I am in no way attempting to infer that you're a bad person if things have gone badly with your family.

As I talked about earlier, it is sometimes difficult for families to cope with changes in your life. This can often lead to problems between the two of you. It is imperative to stick together through tough times like this and remember that you're a team now. Enduring through the awkward and tough situations with your families may seem like too much work now but trust me when I say it will be worth it overall. There will be many times in the future when you will be thankful that you stuck through it and worked things out.

If your one of the lucky ones that gets along great with your in-laws while at the same time your parents love your significant other, then congratulations. This is truly a blessing and you should thank God daily for this. If you're really blessed than your parents will get along well with your in-laws and so forth. If this is not the case, I'm sorry to hear that.... but remember that one day you will be on the other side of this situation. For this reason alone, you should do your best to make sure that both sets of parents have a chance to be involved with your lives and eventually with their grandchildren's lives.

Vacations

"This should be an easy one right, why is this even a topic to discuss at this point?". If this was your reaction than you're partially correct. This should be easy, but the reality is that a very large percentage of Americans never use their allotted vacation time every year. Let me start off by saying that I am not one of these people. I do not understand why some people choose not to take advantage of their vacation time. Vacation is the chance for you to refuel and to spend time with your loved ones. No one has ever been lying on their death bed and uttered the words, "I should have worked more instead of spending time with my family". I know that a career can get busy. I understand that you may want to work hard to provide for your family's future. I get that your job can be demanding, and you've got a lot to do. Your work will always be there when you get back from vacation. If you don't take time off to spend with your family, then they may not be in your future that you have worked so hard to prepare for. Life goes by fast and if you don't take time to stop and smell the roses than you will be missing out on life. This brings me to the point as to why this is an important subject to discuss prior to getting married. If you and your significant other do not agree on the importance of taking time off together than there is a good chance you will begin to drift apart over time.

Before you start with the excuses keep in mind that a vacation doesn't have to mean expensive trips to exotic destinations. Sometimes the most relaxing and rewarding time I have is spent at home just relaxing on the couch with my wife and kids. You and your significant other need to make a deliberate effort to plan and follow through on spending time together. This is true for both vacations and date night which I will cover in more detail later. Spending time together is what keeps your relationship strong. There is no difference if this is time spent together at home around the kitchen table playing a game or basking in the sun on some beach in the Caribbean. Sure, the later will get you a better tan but you get my point. My wife and I have learned the trick of putting things like this on the calendar several months ahead of time. Without planning for vacations in advance it is too easy for the time to slip away. Before you know it, months and years slip away.

Chapter 3

You've found "the one", now propose in a
way that she will never forget.

WILL YOU MARRY ME?

SHANNON & PHIL

Obviously, this chapter is geared more towards the gentleman. As a lady, she deserves to be treated to that romantic fairytale ending, or better yet, beginning that she has dreamed of since her first Disney movie. Ladies... make sure your man knows what your dreams are and don't be content with a half-hearted ill prepared proposal. If your guy doesn't have the desire to sweep you off your feet with a romantic proposal, then the odds are that he will not work that hard at keeping your dreams alive after you're married.

Romance and dreams are not about money. It's about love and adoration for one another. If your worried that she will be upset that you didn't spend money beyond your means, then she is not marrying you for love. Yes ladies, I said it. I truly believe that your dreams should become reality for this part of your life. But if your dreams include breaking the bank than your asking too much and your also not focusing on what truly matters, which is the love and connection between the two of you.

Ladies this is the part where you need to stop reading. I am going to help your prince by tossing a few ideas at him. He can't very well surprise you if you've peeked at his playbook. Just as the groom is not supposed to see the bride before the wedding on the special day you're not supposed to see his plans for proposing before it happens. You're still reading, aren't you? I mean it ...STOP READING NOW and pick this book back up afterwards or jump to chapter 4, you will thank me later.

Now guys, as if I had not already set the bar high enough here is another zinger for you.

She's been planning this day since she was 6, you're going to screw this up somehow.

Before you get too nervous and chicken out, know that there is still hope. If you truly know your lady, then you will know what she has been dreaming about. If you don't then I suggest you start figuring that out. Ask her, talk to her parents, her siblings, her friends. Not only will you learn so much more about who she truly is, but you will also guarantee your success.

All right guys now that we're alone let's get to work. Before you plan anything, you need to truly understand what she wants. Then you need to blow her socks off by making it ten times better. Before you run off and plan some elaborate highly publicized proposal be sure that is what she really wants. It's true that this type of over the top proposal can be romantic and very special but only if she is okay with being the center of attention. Your lady might prefer a more reserved private engagement or one that involves family and friends. What makes a truly spectacular unforgettable proposal is the fact that you understand who she is and what she likes. To help you conquer this seemingly Herculean task I have broken down my suggestions into three distinct groups. Even though you may already have an idea regarding how you want to propose, I suggest reading each of the following paragraphs as many of the ideas are suitable regardless of which style you choose.

- Just the two of us
- Family and friends
- Look honey we're on the Jumbotron

Just the two of us

If your lady is the shy introverted type that hides behind the nearest plant at the first indication of being the center of attention than these suggestions are probably more her speed. Gentlemen don't think for even one minute that you've dodged a bullet and you're going to get off easy here. This just means you must work even harder, so you get all the details just right.

Dinner and movie... don't even think about it.... this is a marriage proposal not a first date. Dinner is a good starting point, but it must be someplace special. Dinner could include something you prepared, a romantic restaurant, dinner on the beach at sunset, alone in the park, underneath the stars overlooking the city, get creative with the location. The more thought you put into selecting the perfect spot the more it will mean to her. Make sure you get help from friends and family on ideas and perhaps even staging the scene. Even though this proposal may just be between the two of you it is still okay to have secret operatives helping things along. For instance, you've found the perfect spot to propose and you want to have a romantic scene setup for dinner or drinks but there is no way you can set the scene yourself without giving away the surprise. Enlist some family or friends to bring all the fixings for a romantic dinner to her favorite spot at a park or on the beach. I am talking about the whole shebang. Tables, chairs, tablecloth, candles, flowers, place settings, 3 course meal, music, champagne, etc. You can even have one or two family or friends stand in as the wait staff. Do you or one of your friends play an instrument or sing? Having one of your friends play violin while both of you eat is a nice touch. There is nothing more romantic and special to a woman than having her guy plan every detail of the perfect proposal. Don't forget, your competing against every romantic movie she's ever seen. You might choose to propose before entering upon the scene as this will no doubt give away your surprise. If your good at playing it up, you might be able to pull off that you stumbled across someone else's romantic scene and be able to drop down on one knee before she figures it out.

Dinner should only be part of your proposal plot. What you really want to do is create an entire day of unforgettable memories. In fact, there are countless options for your engagement day. For example, you can choose to start off the day with a fun activity that the two of you enjoy together and then move onto dinner followed by a romantic walk on the beach. At which point throughout the day you plan to propose is entirely up to you and what you think she will like the best. Don't keep her guessing too long as she may not play along with your plans and want to change things up. This could force to you show your hand and spoil the moment. My personal recommendation would be to plan the proposal for no more than 2 to 3 hours into the date. This is enough time for you to set the scene for romance but not too long that your schedule can get off track and mess with your plans. You will also need to plan accordingly for the activities of the day. Don't take her roller skating through the park and then expect her to be ready for dinner at a formal restaurant an hour later. It's fine to make that part of your plan but be sure to allow ample time for her to get ready. Whatever you do, don't rush her. All the romance in the world will quickly disappear if she is pressed for time.

I have included some more hints about the actual proposal towards the end of this chapter that you should read later but this paragraph is about what to do afterwards. The odds are that even if your bride is shy and was thankful for the very personal proposal she will undoubtedly want to tell somebody about your engagement at this point. This means that you should leave some time at the end of the day for the two of you to visit family and/or friends. You might even want to arrange a small family and friend get together afterwards. This doesn't have to be much, but it will most definitely add to her special day. The fact that everyone else knew about your plans will also make her feel even more special. Be a little cautious here as it is possible to go too over the top with the after party. Try and keep the size appropriate to her level of comfort. If you're not sure that she would be happy with a small get together afterwards than just plan for this sort of thing as an option for her if she's up for it. Once again, the idea is no pressure. Don't stress her out by forcing her into something that she doesn't want to do. All your plans and preparation can be tarnished by enacting an ill-conceived plan. This may seem a bit like a conflicting message, but every person is different and the one person that should know her best is you. If you're not sure what she would like than you have not done your homework and you're not ready for the proposal.

Family and friends

If your reading this paragraph, then you have figured out that your lady would love to share this special moment with family and friends. You have two options with this type of proposal. First, where everybody is in on it ahead of time. Second, where they will be just as surprised as she is.

I would say that the more difficult proposal to pull off would be where no one is wise to your plans, especially if you want them to be in attendance for the proposal. Certainly, this plan is not impossible, but it will take a bit of tact to get everyone together while still making sure the proposal is all about her. You might be okay if this is her birthday party, but I would avoid trying to pull this off at her grandma's 80th birthday celebration. Opening a wedding ring as a gift at the family Christmas party can prove to be very romantic and memorable. However, this day is supposed to be all about her, so you need to be confident that all would be accepting.

If you choose to enlist a few conspirators to help you plan the occasion your options for a unique and truly unforgettable proposal are greatly increased. The events mentioned above could still apply but with help you don't have to coordinate the proposal with some other event as a coverup. I would also say that the venue for the proposal would have a wider range of options as you can have friends and family meet wherever you want. Do yourself a favor and get creative with the venue. The bowling alley where you guys play every week is probably not the best spot. Not to say this is a bad idea but even if she loves bowling it doesn't exactly scream romance. I would also recommend avoiding a bar or club for the same reason. The same goes for her work place. You don't want her to think of her job every time she looks at the rock on her finger. A party at a friend's house can be a great way to get everyone together. You can also consider some more public locations that aren't too busy. We'll save Time Square for the next category. The beach, the gazebo in the park, the lookout spot along your favorite hiking trail, a cabin in the woods, at the base of the Christmas tree near your home town, a botanical garden, on a dinner cruise boat, the top of a tall building, at her favorite coffee shop or café, overlooking the bridge, or at the zoo. Just not in front of the monkeys, you don't need your special moment upstaged by some baboon showing off his backside. There is probably a dozen or more examples and many that are unique to where you live. The important thing to think about here is to put yourself in her shoes for a moment and think of how she would want to reply to the question, "so, where did he propose?" Just a hint gentlemen, the answer she wants to give is not "in the bar next to some drunk" or "the dog food isle at the grocery store".

Regardless of the location make sure her family and friends are part of it. This should also include members of your family and friends as well. You don't necessarily need a large group of people either. It really should be the family and friends that the two of you are closest to. If she has family that is out of town it can be a nice surprise to arrange for them to be there as well. Especially if it's her parents or one of her siblings. I realize that getting married is about the two of you and your future life together, but the importance of family cannot be understated. In some cases, it may not be possible to gather all the people that she would really want to share this moment with and that is okay as well. The key point is that if she is close to her family and friends your engagement and marriage should only strengthen these relationships. If she is not close to her family than it may be important for your family to be there. Marriage means the families are linked together as one larger family that is there to support one other. I realize that I am painting a picture of a utopia that may not seem to exist on the surface. As I touched on previously some family relationships can be trying while some can be downright destructive. With this in mind, I am not suggesting that you use this opportunity to reunite her with family or friends where there is significant tension or issues. This would most likely ruin any special part of the proposal. What I am trying to get at is that you should not exclude any family members simply because they can be a bit difficult at times. This is certainly not the time to bring up issues that you have with her family or friends. In fact, this sort of thing should have been dealt with long before even thinking about the proposal.

Look honey we're on the Jumbotron

As the title of this paragraph eludes, this type of proposal is the kind of stuff you see in the movies. This type of proposal is certainly not for everyone as both of you will certainly be the center of attention for hundreds, perhaps thousands, of complete strangers. These grand gestures of expressing your love and devotion are impactful but they must also be personal and truly heartfelt. If your choosing to propose this way to win her back after doing something stupid, then it will not have the same meaning and it will most likely not erase whatever happened between the two of you. You should only pick this style because you truly cannot picture your life without her in it and you want to shout it from the mountain tops so the whole world knows.

If you want to pull off a truly epic unbelievably romantic proposal that they will write stories about then you are most definitely going to need help. Despite what movies want us to believe a flash mob will not just randomly break out right before you get ready to propose. But if you can pull off organizing enough family or friends to make this happen then you will have created a truly memorable moment that the two of you will share for decades to come. As the title suggests a proposal appearance on the Jumbotron at a game with her favorite sports team is pretty great. However, if you're at a game with your favorite team and she would rather be anywhere else than you kind of missed the mark. As with all the other proposals I have talked about, this is about her, not you. Don't plan any proposal based on what you think would be awesome. This needs to be a proposal that she has been dreaming about since she was young. If this means you need a horse and buggy or a stretch limousine than you had better start planning. I told you this would be epic I didn't say it would be easy.

I have a friend who proposed to his wife in the middle of the skating rink at the center of downtown after he had pre-arranged for the officials to clear the ice of everyone. All this while, unbeknownst to her, both of their families and many of their friends were in the crowd to witness this truly epic expression of love and devotion. He even arranged reservations at a restaurant across from the skating rink for an after party.

You may think it would be way too difficult to arrange for this sort of thing to happen in a very public place. You would be surprised what complete strangers will let you get away with in the name of true love. Everyone enjoys a great love story with a bright future. Don't hesitate to shoot for the stars. I have been married for over 20 years and my only regret is that I didn't plan a grand proposal. Sure, it was romantic, and my wife would say that she loved the way I proposed which is great and why I love her dearly. However, if I could go back 20 years and do it again I would want to give her the fairytale proposal of her dreams. After all, if you're only going to do something once in your life you should make sure it is the best you could do. I don't want to discourage those who have chosen one of the two previous styles because once again this is about her and not you. If she truly would not want an over the top proposal that is what matters.

The proposal

The actual proposal should include more than just "will you marry me?". Obviously, those words need to be included but you should also start with a few of your favorite things about her and how she makes you feel. It's okay to include how beautiful she looks but you also need to mention things about her personality. Mention things about how she supports you, her smile, her warm embrace, her laugh, the way she looks at you, how smart she is, her sense of humor, or really anything that you find alluring about who she is as a person.

It really doesn't matter if you memorize what you're going to say or whether you need to pull out a piece of paper containing your deepest thoughts. You should however spend some time practicing what you're going to say in an attempt to keep you from bumbling over your words when you're nervous. If you do need a cheat sheet just remember to pause frequently so that you can look into her eyes. This of course will not be possible if she has covered her face to hide from all the attention, exactly why you need to do your homework and pick the type of proposal based on her comfort level not yours. I fully realize that this may be asking you to step out of your comfort zone in order pull this off. Like they say, go big or go home. If she knows you well she will understand just how far you were willing to go to express your love for her.

The proposal must also include you getting down on one knee. There are only a few exceptions where I'll let you off the hook on this one. If you're in a helicopter overlooking a massive "will you marry me" sign on the ground or if your underwater with scuba gear while opening a clam with the wedding ring inside, then you can skip the on bended knee thing. Obviously, these are only a couple of examples that would make it nearly impossible for you to get on your knee, but you get what I'm saying. This is important not simply because it's tradition but also because it shows respect and admiration for her. If you think I am making too big of a deal about ensuring this day will be overwhelmingly special for her than you need to go back and re-read this book from chapter one. There will be plenty of times where you can expect her to reciprocate the same kind of admiration towards you, but not today.

It wouldn't be much of a marriage proposal without the ring. I am not going to tell you that it needs to cost as much as three months of your salary or anything like that, but it should not have come from a gum ball machine either. No matter what any women says, they all want to show off their shiny new bling from their fiancé. However, there is a happy median between eating Raman noodles for a year to save up the money and needing a microscope to find the diamond on her finger. If money is tight then opt for a less expensive simple setting with whatever size diamond you can afford. There will always be the opportunity to upgrade the diamond later down the road for an anniversary gift. I am not even going to pretend to be an expert on diamonds and their umpteen levels of grading and quality. Seek professionals to help from a respectable jeweler. It is also a good idea to ask her family and friends for advice on the style of ring she likes. Remember she has been planning this for much of her life and she has talked to someone she is close to about what type of wedding ring she wants from her knight on that white horse.

I just have one more thing to bring up with you before we invite your lady back to the conversation. Now that you have won her over and earned the right to call her your fiancé, the job of sweeping her off her feet is not quite over. In fact, it's just beginning. Trust me when I say this, the happier she is the happier you will be and the more you give to the relationship the more she will give in return. I am not talking about material gifts, sure they are included from time to time, but I am referring to non-material things that can't be bought or sold. These are the things that a real and meaningful relationship is based on.

Open the door for her... car door included. Help her put on her coat. Tell her you love her often and spontaneously. Tell her how beautiful she looks, especially when she just woke up and has no makeup on. Ask her how her day went. Bring her flowers for no reason at all. Text her little sweet nothings out of the blue. Ask her opinion. Get her a blanket when she falls asleep on the couch. Bring her a cup of coffee in the morning. Dance with her every chance you get, even if it's at home with no music playing. Caress her cheek before you kiss her. Rub her feet. Tell her how much she means to you. Give her a hug when she's having a bad day, don't try to fix it, just hug her. This list could go on forever. By now you should get the idea...do everything and anything you can think of to show her how much you love her and how she is your queen.

On the surface these things may seem small and irrelevant but they all add up to become the true expression of your love for her. I promise you that all of this will come back to you tenfold. Women are natural nurturers and most, not all, love to be nurtured as well. This is not about being sexist or any notion that women can't handle things themselves. This is about treating her the same way you will eventually want your daughter treated by her boyfriend/fiancé/ husband.

In the few weeks leading up to the wedding plan something extra special for every day. I brought my wife a red rose every morning for two weeks prior to the wedding. The day before the wedding I brought a white rose to represent how she stands out in a crowd. This of course works but if you can think of something equally romantic, or better, do it. You only get one chance to create the foundation of an everlasting relationship with your wife.

Chapter 4

Welcome back ladies, time to start the wedding plans.

Before I jump into the specifics I have just one more message for the guys. I know you just spent weeks or even months planning the perfect proposal and now you think you've earned the right to sit back and let her take over the wedding plans, this couldn't be further from the truth. From this point on the two of you are a team and everything you do from now till the end of time should be thought of this way. There are going to be certain times or topics where you will switch off leading the team but neither one of you should ever go it alone. This is one of those times where the lady will most likely want to take the reins. With that being said, I will offer a word of caution to the ladies. If your fiancé is unwilling to **happily** support you through the wedding planning stage it is a pretty good indication that there may be similar issues in the future when it comes to parenting, finances, careers, or other critical aspects. For the guys who feel like I just threw them under the bus, grow a pair. Real men support their wife and their families in all aspects of their lives together. I would do nothing less for the love of my life and I certainly would not sit idly by while my daughters were treated any differently.

Wedding planning

I am not going to lie to you and say there is an easy stress-free method for planning your wedding. Frankly I am not an expert on the details of planning these events. Nor am I going to pretend that I can do it any better than the hundreds of magazines, web pages, or planning services available today. Instead I would like to offer a few words of advice on how to handle the stress, decisions, compromises, and disagreements that will inevitably pop up throughout the process. To start with, both of you need to remember three of the most important things.

1) Trust in God, if you put your trust in Him he will provide for you.

2) Trust in each other, all relationships, personal and professional, are built on trust. If you can't rely on and trust your fiancé than you should not be getting married in the first place.

3) Keep your family close and always treat them with the same respect and gratitude you would like in return. Family is a bond that can never be broken regardless of how strained it may get at times.

All three of these things require faith on your part. This can be difficult for some people to do as most people are more comfortable when things are in their control. This is in fact something that was particularly difficult for me to do. Once you realize the fact that it will only help you overall it is much easier to accept.

One thing to help you deal with the stress is to remember why you're getting married in the first place. It's about love and a long lasting meaningful relationship. Looking at it this way can help you to overlook some of the details that are not turning out the way you had originally planned or hoped.

Keeping in mind that both of you will be stressed at times it critically important to be cognitive in recognizing when your fiancé is stressed. As their partner in life it is your job to be understanding, comforting, and helpful during these times. It also critical for you to recognize when your stressed and to let your fiancé and family know so they can be there to help. Some people are better at hiding stress while others are just not good at recognizing it in themselves or others. These things work both ways. A relationship founded on the ability to **read** other's emotions through body language and subtle tells is one that will undoubtedly be a very rewarding and happy marriage. Many people, particularly guys, are not always good at picking up on these subtle clues. While you're getting to know each other, the first 3-5 years (longer for some), it is important to verbalize your emotions more often so that your partner knows what to look for in the future. Please do not interpret **verbalize** to mean scream and yell. I get that your probably frustrated and stressed but you can draw a parallel to training a dog, you don't want your wife/husband to run into the other room every time you lose your cool. If you help them to better identify when your stressed they can be there to help you in the future before you get to the breaking point. This is a much better alternative to having them wet themselves on the living room floor when you raise your voice. Hopefully this is only a problem with your dog, but you get the idea.

The big day

It's finally here, months or even years in the making, this is the time you have been planning for and anticipating. The biggest piece of advice I can provide on this day is to relax and breath. It will all be okay and whatever happens it will not matter down the road as long as the two of you are there for each other.

With the very real possibility of scaring you I will tell you that it is nearly impossible for everything to go as planned on your wedding day. Therefore, it is important to stay focused on the why and not the how of getting married. My intention here is not to scare you but it is better to be prepared than to be surprised. It is a very good idea to surround yourself with your family and friends that can help if something starts to stray off course.

If you have some friends or family that don't handle stress well than it might be in your best interest to assign them roles that are least likely to encounter problems. This may sound bad at first but if you're worried about one of your family members becoming the issue than you might want to secretly assign a handler to this individual in advance. Having someone to help manage their stress will help to reduce your stress. It doesn't mean that this person is any less loved, in fact by having someone there to help with their stress shows you care. You may not want to let them know you have assigned them a "handler" but you can tell them "so and so" has volunteered to be their helper for the day. Picking a helper for them is nowhere near as funny as assigning them a handler but it will most likely be more well received by that person.

Probably the second biggest piece of advice I can offer on your wedding day is make sure that you and your fiancé have agreed to not drink too much alcohol. A glass of wine or one beer may help take the edge off and reduce stress but getting plastered at your wedding is not only tacky, but it is a horrible way to start off your marriage. Don't take the chance of missing out on these memories that will last forever. I wish I didn't even have to bring this up, but it happens way too often for me not to mention. As it is you will probably wind up with one of your friends or relatives who will not be able to resist the jackpot that is an open bar. It might even be a good idea to have a cash bar for alcohol as this will cut down on your costs and reduce the chance of someone overdoing it. If someone complains, that's their problem, just tell them you had to reduce costs somewhere. Frankly, you don't need to pay for someone to tarnish your wedding night with a drunken display of stupidity.

Honeymoon time

If your reading this than you've made it past the dating, meeting the family, the proposal, the planning, and the pinnacle .... your wedding day. Either that or your reading ahead ... which is okay too. Now is the time to start the rest of your lives together. I will start off with congratulations to the both of you! Now that you can call each other husband and wife you get the chance to celebrate with just the two of you. It's time to relax, kick back, and enjoy each other's company. Start out by picking a vacation that both of you will enjoy and consider making it a slow pace trip. After all, the two of you have just finished months of planning and rushing. A backpacking trip through The Grand Canyon or 5 cities in 7 days can be great but it may not give you enough time with each other to unwind and truly enjoy being alone together. Consider instead a schedule where you can pick a few days out of the trip where you decide to do nothing all day except stay in bed till late morning, take long walks, and watch the sunset in each other's arms.

I have seen some couples who have opted to postpone the honeymoon since they spent all their money on the wedding. Although this is not a terrible idea I would strongly advise against it. Life gets busy quickly. Careers, family, buying a home, and possibly even children, will all come around and before you know it you are celebrating your one-year anniversary. If money is tight than consider spending a little less on the wedding so that you have some left over for the honeymoon. Also, there is nothing that says that your honeymoon must be something expensive or far away from home. Your honeymoon should however be just the two of you away from home and work without the normal day to day distractions. You do not want to look back years from now and regret having never taken your honeymoon. We will discuss later the importance of 2nd honeymoons but if you can avoid it don't let you're your first honeymoon seem like your second by putting it off. Even though 2nd, 3rd, and beyond honeymoons are wonderful there is something special about being on your honeymoon as newlyweds.

Chapter 5

The honeymoon is over, now what?

Don't be discouraged by the title of this chapter. I can honestly say that the love I have for my wife has grown more intense every year as our relationship continues to grow even stronger and more rewarding. I can also tell you that this has not happened by accident. Marriage is a commitment that requires long term learning, hard work, and dedication. This chapter is written with the intent to equip both of you with some of the tools and lessons that my wife and I have learned over the years. These tools will help both of you to build upon your relationship so that you can fan the flame that ignites your love. The goal is to turn that flame into an eternal flame that can survive any storm that life may throw your way.

Fundamentals of a Good Marriage

Trust

By now I have probably mentioned trust a dozen times or so ... actually 16 times before this chapter, I checked just in case anybody was keeping track. There is good reason for this as trust is the foundation of any relationship, personal or business. Ideally you would have been able to work through any trust issues early in your relationship, hopefully even before getting engaged. If not, it certainly is one of the first items to address now. Chapters 1 and 2 get into this topic extensively and although they are written from the viewpoint of being boyfriend/girlfriend most of the advice is still valid for married couples. The one big distinction here is that although breaking up is a suitable option when you're dating, it is absolutely NOT an option you should consider once you're married. There may be a few reasons where separation might be the only workable solution to marital problems, but it should only be considered after every other option has been fully exhausted. I will talk more on this in chapter 9.

To be 100% clear on this topic I wanted to take a quick moment and talk about trust itself. The reason I feel this is important is that I do not believe people place enough emphasis on trust nowadays as they should. In the not too distant past, trust was as good as gold. Being able to trust someone meant you could count on them to follow through on their promise regardless of the circumstances. Too many people these days throw around the word as if the word itself establishes it's meaning. Simply saying "trust me" in no way fulfills the magnitude of truly being able to trust someone. Let me start with a wild and crazy example that would never happen but it's so outlandish that it should make my point clear. If someone offered my wife $500million dollars to cheat on me with them, I know, without any doubt, that I could trust her to not even consider the notion. The point of this statement is not how much money it would take, but the fact that no amount of money would be enough for my wife or myself to compromise our relationship in any way. This doesn't mean that my wife and I don't get jealous or question each other from time to time. We are human like everybody else and we fall victim to moments of insecurity and doubt. However, the best part of our relationship is that we have no secrets from each other and that all aspects of our life are fair game. Any moment of insecurity can be quickly quenched by simply asking the other.

Trust is what enables a relationship to truly grow on a level that is not possible without it. It is not only trust regarding faithfulness, but also trust in all other aspects of life. For example, I know without question that if I were to become ill or disabled in anyway my wife would be by my bedside for the rest of our lives. I would do the same for her in return. This kind of trust allows you to let go of the things that cause you fear or worry. Life can be pretty trying at times, but unrelenting trust in your spouse helps to make it not so scary. Trust encompasses every aspect of your relationship together. Knowing that your spouse will not squander the rent money on alcohol, gambling, shopping sprees, frivolous trips, or new electronic gadgets is just as important. It's trust in your spouse that they will come to you with important decisions that affect your life together. Nobody wants to be surprised by their spouse dropping the bomb that they just accepted a promotion requiring the two of you need to move to Timbuktu. Actual city by the way, I used to think it was just something someone made up. Anyway, it doesn't mean that you wouldn't be just as excited as them, but it's certainly something that should be discussed first so that you can decide together. This example leads directly into the next topic which is communication.

Communication, communication, communication

Just because you've heard everyone preaching that good communication is the key to a good relationship doesn't mean that you will put it into practice. The biggest reason for this is that communication is only about 10% of what you say verbally. The other 90% is what you do and how you say it. Any parent with a teenager can tell you that the words "I'm sorry", muttered from the mouth of a clearly annoyed, utterly aggravated, disgruntled adolescent does not really mean "I'm sorry". In fact, they might as well have just said, "whatever gets you out of my face right now because I hate you". If you think I'm exaggerating, just wait till you have a teenager, you'll see. Saying the words doesn't really carry any weight unless it's sincere and you back it up with actions.

Showing your love and devotion to your spouse is more than just flowers and candy. Let's take a short trip back to your childhood for a moment. I think that most people would agree that their mother loved them. Based on this preposition, as a child how do you know that your mother loved you? Is it because she took care of you when you were sick or because she made your lunch for school? Is it because she held you when you were scared and laughed with you when you were happy? Is it because she washed your clothes and helped you with your homework? Is it because she bought you things for no reason and how she drove you and your friends everywhere you wanted to go? The answer to all these questions is undoubtedly yes. Although the relationship between you and your spouse should in no way be compared to that between you and your mother, the ways in which your love is expressed should be very much the same.

Showing your love for your spouse means taking them to a dozen clothing stores to find that perfect dress even though she will totally disregard your opinion on how she looks awesome in every single one she tried on. Complaining the entire time does not count and in fact, completely negates it.

Showing your love means letting your husband and his stinky friends hang out in your living room for hours watching the football game or playing some childish video game. Once a week is love, every day is not a marriage.

Showing your love is cleaning the house and taking care of the dishes before she gets home.

Showing your love is buying his favorite snack and soft drink so that he can sit down after a hard day and relax.

Showing your love is coming in the door after a long day and spending the first fifteen minutes asking her how her day was, just listening to what's on her mind.

Showing your love is going to see the latest action blockbuster even though you had your heart set on the romantic comedy. This works both ways, compromise is part of good communication.

Showing your love is sitting down on the couch to watch tv together while rubbing her feet with lotion. Just because you want her to relax, not because she asked you.

Showing your love is going to his friend's house for a party even when you would rather just stay home.

Showing your love is not just letting her, but also encouraging her, to go hang out with her friends. Once again, one or two times a week is healthy, much more than that might be a problem. Obviously, like all the rest of these, this works both ways.

Showing your love is biting your tongue when her mother makes some aggravating remark directed at you. I can say this because my mother-in-law is wonderful and never says what's truly on her mind. Bit of inside joke for my mother-in-law, whom I truly cherish.

I could sit here for days or even weeks and write about the different ways to show your love for your spouse. In general, anything you do for your spouse simply because you know it will make them happy is an expression of your love. Keep in mind that it is not a few big gestures but rather many small acts that happen over time. Big gestures are great and very important for a healthy relationship, but they generally do not happen too often, and they also do not take the place of all the small things that should happen daily.

You're probably thinking that I wandered way of topic talking about showing your love instead of staying true to the heading of communication. What you need to realize is that these actions speak so much louder and clearer than words ever could. I am treading a bit on dangerous ground here because actual conversation is absolutely essential to good communication. The difference is that the 10% of verbal communication will be indescribably more beneficial if the other 90% of non-verbal communication is good or even great. Let's look at another analogy, putting a brand-new coat of paint on a hundred-year-old house doesn't make the house livable if the foundation is crumbling. Sure, the house may look better for now but without addressing the foundation issues you won't be living there for long.

Now that you have begun to lay the foundation of good marriage we need to talk about the verbal communication between you and your spouse. I have heard from many different sources that you should listen more than you talk. Some say it should be 60% listening and 40% talking while others say 70 or even 80% listening. In reality, the numbers don't matter. What matters is that if both of you are talking more than half the time, than there is a good chance that a large portion of what your saying is going unheard. If both of you practice listening 60% of the time, then there should be 20% of silence which is not a bad thing. For those of you not good at math, just trust me, it's 20%. Anyway, the point is that if you're not listening to what your spouse is saying than how can you expect them to listen to you. Also, when I say listen I mean truly listening, not thinking of your response or what you want for dinner.... tacos or roast beef?....hmmm. Take the time and listen to what they have to say. After all, this is what you want in return. Do I need to quote scripture? "Therefore, whatever you desire for men to do to you, you shall also do to them; for this is the law and the prophets" (Matthew 7:12 KJV).

The biggest problem with verbal communication is that it can be very easy to interpret incorrectly. Let's face it, even if a man and a woman both speak the same language, it doesn't mean that everything that comes out of their mouth will be heard the way it was intended. A good portion of what comes out of my mouth doesn't even make sense to me sometimes. It is human nature to become defensive and spout "that's not what I said" and expect the other person to just suddenly get what you were trying to say. There are many reasons why people interpret what you said differently. It can be due to being in a different state of mind, different upbringing, different dialects, miss hearing you, or just plainly not understanding what you meant. It is much more effective to respond with "that's not what I meant" followed by a different explanation of your intent.

Just like all other parts of a marriage, communication is give and take and it requires effort from both sides to be effective. The biggest thing to remember is to give the benefit of the doubt to your spouse when having a conversation. Avoid getting upset when you first hear something that makes you want to jump out of your skin. Instead of getting angry, ask for clarification. This can be done in several ways but simply asking them to repeat themselves may not be the best as this is what caused concern in the first place. Try rephrasing the statement and asking them if that is what they meant. Be careful not to go to extreme. After all, "I would like to see someone else", means something totally different when their referring to getting a second opinion from another doctor. Responding with, "fine I want a divorce too", might be taking it a bit too far. This might be a drastic example but how many times have you ended an argument where neither of you even remember how it started.

You shouldn't say anything to your spouse unless you truly mean it. Perhaps the only exception to this is actually telling your spouse you love them even if your upset with them at that moment. It's okay to say, "I love you, but I am still upset with you". Honestly this is one of the best ways to diffuse an argument. It's difficult to keep yelling at someone who just said they love you. This in no way should end the conversation as the reason you were having an argument still needs to be discussed. Keep in mind, disagreements are rarely resolved through yelling at each other.

The last couple of paragraphs have included suggestions for avoiding and possibly ending arguments. In a perfect world your marriage would avoid them altogether, however, this is highly unlikely. If you engage in healthy conversation and practice non-verbal communication the frequency and intensity of your arguments will diminish over time. I can honestly not remember the last time my wife and had an argument. Not to say we have not had disagreements. For those of you who think I am just trying find a less intense word for argument, let me explain what I mean. Arguments usually start with a disagreement and then end up with yelling and slamming doors. A disagreement is simply a topic where the two of you do not share the same point of view. You can disagree about what to have for dinner, but it doesn't have end with someone wearing the entrée. Disagreements are going to happen in a marriage. If both of you agreed completely on everything it would be a bit freaky.... Just kidding. If you rarely disagree than that is great but, in most cases, there will be many points where the two of you will need to rely on good healthy communication and compromise to resolve differences of opinion. No matter how much I insist that my opinion is a fact, it truly is just my opinion and it may not be the right opinion for the situation. I purposely used "I" in the previous sentence because from time to time we are all guilty of thinking our way is the only way.

Don't sweat the small things, but don't ignore them either.

As all of us grow up and become independent we inevitably develop little habits and idiosyncrasies that, although completely harmless, will tend to secretly and slowly drive our spouses to the brink of nuclear war. These little habits can be as simple as never putting down the toilet seat or leaving wet towels on the bed. It can be leaving the cap off the tooth paste or chewing with your mouth open. These habits can also be a little more noticeable like cutting off people mid-sentence or leaving your underwear where ever it lands. Most of these things will never be noticed while your dating or they may even be overlooked because you were afraid to mention them for fear of hurting their feelings. At this point you might be thinking, "wow his wife must have to walk on eggshells around him." This couldn't be further from the truth. The fact is that after you have lived with someone day in and day out these little habits may begin to slowly eat away at your patience for this relatively benign behavior. It is much better to address this concern with your spouse before that one day comes when you can no longer take it and explode on them like a volcano. Often these little things will come up during another unrelated argument or they can even be the trigger for a much bigger argument. This is especially true if there are multiple items that have bubbled up over time. If you never mention that this behavior bothers you than your spouse will have no idea they are doing something that drives you crazy. It is much better to address these issues when they are small annoyances before they brew into something much bigger. I am going to revert back to an old saying that I learned from my grandmother.

"A stitch in time saves nine." (Proverb)

Basically, if you stop and repair a tear in your shirt when it only requires one or two stitches it will save you from having to make a much larger repair later. By addressing these small issues as they come up it may be possible to avoid a much larger issue further down the road.

As with most things, this can be taken too far as well. At some point your helpful reminders become nagging. Nagging happens to also be one of those idiosyncrasies that can drive your spouse nuts. It is also important to note that your spouse will not drop that annoying habit the first time you bring it up. Instead the two of you should collectively agree to both work on 1 or 2 things at a time that bother each other. With both of you agreeing to work on changing things it will improve your relationship and your communication. Without compromise you are more likely to create a one-sided point of contention between the two of you. Try putting a dollar in a jar every time either of you get caught in the act of your annoying habit. Once both of have gone a few months without having to pay up you can empty the jar and use that money to go out on a date. Handling things this way can create a more playful and constructive atmosphere that is more likely to resolve issues rather than create new problems. You might find that these little habits become great memories that bring the two of you closer.

It is entirely reasonable that instead of working on annoying habits you might find there are a few things that you wish your spouse would do more of. Perhaps you would like your husband to be more affectionate towards you or maybe you would like your wife to wear her hair a certain way more often. There are bound to be a few things that you would like to add or remove from your relationship. There is absolutely nothing wrong with this and it should not be viewed as trying to change the other person. As I talked about earlier, expressing your love for your spouse means you are willing to go to great lengths to make them as happy as you possibly can. If both of you truly share this principal than your relationship will be unbreakable. Your commitment to each other is more important than your own selfish desires. Keep in mind that, once again, this is a two-way street. There is a healthy balance between each of you going the extra mile for one another versus trying to change who you are just to please your spouse.

The fact is that if both of you are more concerned with each other's happiness than with your own happiness, both of you will truly be happy together.

I don't want to belabor this point to death, but I believe it is paramount for a truly happy marriage. Think about it this way, if you do everything you can to make sure your spouse is happy than they will most likely be happy. If your spouse does the same for you then you should be equally as happy. The result being that both of you are happy, but you are only happy because you are together. The principal is simple, if you create a relationship where both of you make each other happy than the mere thought of doing anything to jeopardize that happiness is inconceivable.

Flowers are not just for saying I'm sorry

Sending flowers to your spouse at work is considered one of the most romantic things you can do. However, If the only time you give flowers is when you did something wrong or after an argument, then receiving flowers quickly goes from being romantic to becoming reminiscent about what went wrong. Eventually the sight of you bringing them flowers will trigger them to ask, "what did you do now?" rather than them being filled with joy. Obviously, the flowers in this example can be replaced with a range of many material things. The big idea is that flowers or whatever should be reserved for putting a smile on your spouse's face. This gesture should not be used as a means of avoiding the real issue which is working to address what caused the problem between the two of you. The best way to say "I'm sorry" is by not doing the thing that prompted the need for you to say "I'm sorry" in the first place.

Let's consider the following example. If your best friend punched you in the face followed by a heartfelt apology you might be more likely to forgive them if they didn't turn around and punch you in the face again. Much like the concept of trust that we talked about earlier, the words "I'm sorry" are just words unless their backed up by actions that truly show your sorry.

To a lesser extent, always buying flowers, or candy, or jewelry for a specific date can diminish the meaning of the gesture if that is the only time you express your love this way. Having flowers delivered to their work every year on their birthday is great but receiving flowers on some random Tuesday in the middle June just because your spouse was thinking of you is priceless. Once again, the actual material item is irrelevant as it is just a symbol of your love and devotion to your spouse. Every once in a while, picking up their favorite whatever on the way home is just another way to express your love. The more random the better. Bringing flowers home every Friday is great until the one day you forget. As important as it is to be random and spontaneous it is equally important to do this stuff frequently. Every six months is not enough, every day is both impractical and probably overkill. If you can't remember the last time you did this, shame on you, put down this book now and go get them something. It doesn't have to be expensive. In fact, it could be as simple as leaving a note on the bathroom mirror for them to find, I'm referring to a love note not a reminder to buy toothpaste.

Know your own faults

One of your responsibilities as a spouse is to know your own faults and to strive towards fixing them. I am not referring to physical aspects of yourself that you don't like. These are not faults but rather Gods way of making each one of us unique in our own right. Rather, I am referring to bad habits, social interactions, unhealthy behaviors, quick or hot temperament, and many other personal traits that we all have to some degree. The intent of this section is not to point out your faults or to create self-pity, depression, or demotivation. The point is to take some time for self-reflection on what you would like to change about yourself. Everybody has some behavior they would like to change about themselves. Perhaps you would like to increase your patience or expand your knowledge. Some people want to learn how to be more socially outgoing. Others realize they have some rather self-destructive habits such as drinking too much, smoking, or eating unhealthily. At this point you have probably noticed that it seems I have wondered off course again, after all this is a book about marriage not a self-help book. This brings us to why this topic is relevant for this chapter. Change of any kind can be very difficult to cope with and even more difficult to tackle within yourself without some outside assistance. The good news is that you don't have to take this on all by yourself. In fact, you were lucky enough to find someone special to marry you despite all the things you dislike about yourself. Please note I said things you dislike about **yourself**. I am in no way implying that your so messed up that it is a down right amazing that you found someone to overlook all your faults. That may be true but I'm not implying it.

   Throughout most of my childhood I was shy, reserved, and generally anti-social. I genuinely did not like this part of who I was. It's not that there was something wrong with who I was, but I would become almost crippled in social interactions. As I got older and into high school I realized that much of what I disliked about my behavior was also at least partially responsible for why I spent most of my schooling being teased and bullied. I also realized that it was not my fault that I was being teased but my social interactions with others meant I didn't fit in with most of my peers. Late in high school I was able to muster up enough confidence to individually ask each of my bullies why they teased me so much. What I learned was very shocking to me. Almost every one of them said it was because I acted like I was better than them, they thought I was conceded and overly confident. This shocked me so tremendously because from my perspective things were very much the opposite. I was petrified by the "in crowd", I felt like there was no way they would ever except me into their group. I realized that the only way things would ever change for me would be if I took on the challenge of changing this part of who I was. A few years passed with me slowly working on what I wanted to change about myself and then about half way through my second semester as a freshman in college something happened that I once thought was completely impossible. This single event shocked me so amazingly that I still can't believe it happened this way. After years of having difficulty making friends and being on the outside I was finally part of larger group of friends. To me this was awesome, and I was extremely happy with what I had achieved. The crazy thing is that this is not the amazing moment that I am referring to. I was talking to a friend that I had met in college about how I had made a transformation in myself and how happy I was to have such a great group of friends now. The real shocker was what he told me next. He went on to tell me that he had noticed early in freshman year how outgoing I was and how I was the popular guy that everyone, including himself, wanted to be friends with me. What …I was absolutely stunned that I had gone from the "geek" who everybody teased to the guy that everyone wanted to become friends with.

This transformation was not easy, but it was also not the end of my journey, nor was it the part that changed my life. I still wasn't completely comfortable in social situations and I knew I wanted to do better but I didn't really know how. What happened next in my journey can only be described as a gift from God himself. I walked into my boss's office at work where I stumbled across an angel with golden blonde curly hair. I instantly knew that this angel was someone that I had to know better. That is the moment that truly changed my life as I had just met the woman of my dreams, the woman who would later say yes to my marriage proposal, and the woman whom with I would exchange vows with less than 18 months from that epic day. Twenty years later I honestly look back at my life and realize that the transformation I had made before I met her was just the beginning of becoming the man I am today. With my wife by my side I have been able to continuously challenge myself to become a better person. The best part is that I no longer must go it alone. More importantly, I also am not just doing it for myself either. I continue to challenge myself to become a better person, not because she asked me to but because she deserves the best of who I can be.

Now that I have paused to wipe away my tears of joy I can get back to what I am trying to say. One of the best ways to further entangle your soul with that of your loving spouse is to embark on a journey together of self-betterment. Helping each other every step of the way and knowing the entire time that both of you are working on yourselves for the sake of cementing a better marriage is an indescribable emotion. Before I give you too much of an impression that it's easy let me start by saying that looking at who you are and what you don't like about yourself is difficult, doing something about it is really, really hard. Doing it alone is nearly impossible, especially if you are not doing it for anyone but yourself. Deciding to eat healthier or to stop swearing like a drunken sailor becomes more manageable when you have your spouse to hold you accountable and to offer encouragement to help make it happen. It is usually much better if both of you each agree to work on 1 or 2 things at a time. Biting off too much at once can be overwhelming and make the chance of failure much more likely. Going it alone may be possible but encouragement in the form of your spouse also working on themselves is unparalleled.

If your spouse chooses not to work on anything you should not let this stop you from doing it for yourself and for your marriage. It might be that your spouse will need some encouragement in the form of watching you attain your goals before their ready to commit. For this reason, you should make your spouse aware of your goal and enlist them to hold you accountable towards achieving it. I know this is one sided and completely against one of the fundamentals regarding compromise but sometimes leadership is more powerful inspiration than anything else. If nothing else, you will be happier with who you are as a person once you have reached your goal. Referring back to an earlier chapter in this book, a person must want to change in order for change to be successful. Forcing someone to change almost never works long term. Some people have a harder time admitting to themselves and especially to others that they are not perfect. The reality is that NO human is, was, or will ever be perfect as long as they're still living among us mere mortals. All we can ever hope to do is to become better people that are more caring, loving, forgiving, friendly, compassionate, selfless, truthful, giving, nurturing, patient, thankful, passionate, enduring, and genuine. It is also entirely possible that you need to look deeper within yourself when you find fault with others. Be certain that there isn't something that you need to change within you rather than something they need to work on. Many times, our own impatience or unrealistic expectations are in fact the real issue, rather than anything the other person maybe doing or not doing. With that being said, there are also many cases where the issue truly lies with the other person. This problem is more challenging to overcome, and it can be very destructive to your relationship. If you feel your spouse is doing something destructive towards your marriage or towards themselves that they need to change this topic will be covered later in chapter 9.

Chapter 6

Sex after marriage, yes men it does exist, and
if your meeting her needs she'll meet yours.

I know that both of my daughters are cringing at the very thought of me talking about sex. I felt the same way if the topic was ever brought up with my mother as well. However, I have no problem talking about sex as it is an extremely important part to having a truly happy marriage. Having an intimate relationship with your spouse is crucial. Regardless of your opinion the fact is that intimacy is the difference between what constitutes a marriage and other relationships. Not having sex with your spouse can be almost as damaging to the relationship as being unfaithful. Before I venture down this road any further I will make it undoubtably clear from the very beginning that there is absolutely NO excuse for being unfaithful to your spouse. This includes lack of sex between the two of you as well as unfaithfulness of your spouse. You heard me right, two wrongs do not make a right and that certainly applies to being faithful.

Romance novels are not a phenomenon because women hate sex, if you're not getting any it's most likely because you're not making her happy outside the bedroom.

Intimacy and making love has brought my wife and I emotionally closer together over the years. I have heard many people complain and joke that there is no such thing as sex after marriage. If that is your reality than you're doing "it" wrong. I am not talking about learning some new tricks from the 'Kamasutra' or '50 Shades of Grey'. I am talking about connecting on an emotional level that will keep your sex life exciting for years to come.

For women intimacy starts before you climb into bed with the other person. It also did not start 10 minutes earlier when you smacked her butt in the bathroom. The intimacy started for her when you woke up this morning and emptied the dishwasher before you left for work. It started when you texted her in the middle of the day just to say, "I love you". It started when you picked up a loaf bread and a gallon of milk on your way home like she asked you to do. It started when she walked in the door and you asked her how her day went. It started last week when you rubbed her feet while the two of you were watching TV together. It started last month when you picked her mother up and drove her to the doctor's office. It started when you did all the little things that shows her how much you love her and how much you care for her and her happiness. For women it's not just about the act of being physical, that's certainly part of it, but it's more about what makes "chick flicks" popular.

Guys are simple, sex is sex, and we could care less if she just yelled at us for leaving the toilet seat up. We are not going to turn her down because we're "just not feeling it tonight". I am not saying that guys don't appreciate or need all those other moments of her expressing her love, it's just not a factor we consider when it comes to sex. I know it may sound very animalistic and I will probably catch all kinds of flack for being so candid about it but for the most part it's pretty much reality. It's just the way guys are wired, we think about sex at least a half a dozen times a day and most guys I know would not consider it too much to have sex more than once a day.

It is not that women don't enjoy sex, once again dirty romance novels and the Bachelor don't exist because they could do without. The difference for them is that sex is very much tied to the emotional connection between the two of you. This connection is there for guys but to a significantly lesser amount. This has been the case for thousands of years and I don't suspect it will change anytime soon. Sure, my statements are very stereotypical and obviously the degree to which these statements apply to any individual will vary but the basis is very true. Knowing and accepting these stereotypes as reality will make your love life much better as it is about connecting with your spouse on the level that is right for both of you.

Sorry women sex once a month is not enough.

That's right ladies, just as you wouldn't be content with him expressing his love for you once a month he will not be content with having sex only once a month. I am not saying that the exchange is one for one, this is not a swap meet, it's a relationship that requires, communication, and compromise. The frequency with which you have sex should be something that both of you are happy with. If that's once a week so be it, if it's every other day, good for you both. I am not one to kiss and tell but I will say that even after twenty years of marriage, I am a very very happy man. I realized I just grossed out both my daughters, but they'll get over it.

As I probably just ticked off half of the women reading this book I want to point something out first. I started this chapter off speaking to the men as I am under no disillusion that most guys are not doing what they should. I realize that you women are probably giving more than your getting in return. In no way am I suggesting that if you give him more of what he wants that you will automatically get what you're longing for. Honestly, because most men don't think this way they will most likely not figure it out by themselves. Like I said guys are pretty simple regarding this and they tend not to see the connection between these things. This is where communication and compromise come into play. Sometimes guys need to be told directly and very clearly what you're looking for. I know this is not fair to you ladies and I would apologize on behalf of all men if I thought that would make a difference. I strongly believe that most guys need to step up their game and take better care of their wives. Unfortunately, I can't reach out of this book and smack some sense into him. This must fall back to you to teach him, not the smacking…the attentiveness, if his parents failed to instill this within him. I will also tell you something that you are most keenly aware of, you ladies hold all the cards. I'm not suggesting withholding sex will help, this may in fact just cause more issues. However, as you might agree, most guys are dogs and dogs can be trained using positive reinforcement. Don't take that the wrong way. I am merely suggesting that through communication and compromise you can both get what you want. You will also likely discover that you and your husband will grow emotionally closer together as a result.

Guys, a keg does not take the place of a six pack. Don't get one and expect her to stay a size 8.

Almost everybody I know has gained at least some weight after getting married. This is completely normal for both of you. It is generally a sign that you have grown comfortable with each other. 10-20lbs is really nothing to be concerned with but beyond that it might be a sign that you're getting a bit too comfortable. The biggest double standard I see is that the husband puts on 20-30lbs and expects his wife to stay the same as the day they got married. Come on guys you wouldn't be okay with this if it was the other way around so don't let this happen.   I am not suggesting that either one of you should let your weight get out of control. The reason for this is for much more than just looks. Staying healthy should be a priority for both of you. Keep in mind the vows that the two of you shared, "In sickness and health, till death do us part". What this means is that the decisions you make now affect both of you instead of just yourself. If you make the choice to let your health suffer than your spouse will now have more concerns regarding what to do if something happens to you. This compounds even further after the two of have decided to have children. From that point on your decisions affect everybody in your family, not just you and your spouse. I may not be in as good shape as the day we got married but I see it as a responsibility to my wife and my daughters to do what I can to stay healthy for their sake.

One of the other concerns that is at least equally as important, if not more so, is your own self confidence. Your spouse married you because of who you are not just how you look. If you start to lose your self-confidence you will inevitably begin to also lose part of who you are as a person. This can impact how you act and what you enjoy doing. The most dangerous part about this is that you may not even notice these changes in yourself. Your spouse will most definitely notice these subtle changes, but they will most likely not understand the cause. The first couple years of marriage can be a bit tricky. Both of you are learning more about each other and settling into your new life together. Mixing in other variables such as these can put unnecessary stress on your relationship that may be difficult to recover from. This may seem like I am putting even more stress on you. What I am attempting to do is assist in building your awareness with the hope that you can identify this type of behavior in either yourself or your spouse. Simply identifying what is happening doesn't immediately remedy the circumstances but it certainly is the most critical step towards addressing them. It's the difference between repairing a small leak in your roof versus your ceiling collapsing due to prolonged water damage. Over time that small drip can cause real damage that is much harder to fix. All of us go through changes and varying levels of self-confidence throughout our lives, after all, this is part of getting older and wiser. The good news is that as the years progress in your marriage you will both get better at identifying changes in each other and you will also get better at helping each other through rougher times. The trick is being able to continually develop your relationship so that the two of you grow and change together over the years. Too much change that happens too quickly can be very dangerous. This especially true if only one of you is changing or if your both changing in different directions.

Chapter 7

Children... the most terrifying, yet incredibly wonderful thing you will ever do in your life.

My biggest challenge for this chapter will be to finish writing it without having to stop every couple of sentences to dry my tears. The entire reason I began this book was for the benefit of my two precious daughters. For that reason alone, this will most likely be the most turbulent chapter as I swing between the brink of tears for the love of my daughters and intense outrage regarding the horrific examples of inexcusably terrible parenting I have witnessed from so called parents.

All children are born pure of heart, perfectly innocent, and 100% reliant on their parents for everything. There is no job on this planet or beyond that is more important than raising your children the best possible way that you can. After God, they are undoubtably the single most important person in both your lives. With this great responsibility comes some incredible challenges but it also comes with indescribable rewards...I didn't even make it through the second paragraph without tearing up.

If you thought that getting married required you to give up your selfish ways, then you're in for a real surprise when it comes to being a parent. From the very minute you first discover that you're going to become a father or a mother your entire perspective on life will begin to change. It will soon no longer matter what your friends are planning for the weekend. Getting your hands on the latest smartphone will become a distant thought as your focus shifts towards preparing your world for the birth of your child. It's not to say that these wants and desires will immediately and completely disappear, but they will however take a back seat compared to the wellbeing of your child.

It's time for one of those rants that I warned you about. If you or your spouse are not entirely ready and undoubtably willing to put your wants and desires behind those of your future children than please strongly consider waiting to have your first child. Raising a child in an environment where one or both parents have not fully matured themselves can be very traumatic and unhealthy for both the child and the marriage. If your already past the point of no return, already pregnant for those of you not keen to my subtle hint towards my utter lack of tolerance for abortion, then you and your spouse have about nine months to finish growing up. I will make no apologies for my harsh tone here. Every time I see a child who is mistreated or even put second place behind either one of their parents I want to lash out irrationally. For those of you considering abortion as an option I beg you to consider giving your child up for adoption as an alternative. There are so many loving would be parents in this world that would do almost anything to have a child. There really is no acceptable reason why you should not go this route. I know people who have regretted their decision to have received an abortion, this is something that time cannot heal. Rant over...at least for now.

The first couple of years with your child will undoubtedly seem like some of the most trying times of your life. Enjoy every moment of this time with your children as all to soon they will be adolescents and you will find yourself missing the baby years. It's not to say that any stage of your child's journey to adulthood is any better or more trying than any other, I truly have enjoyed every single stage of my daughters' lives. At each stage you will find yourself both grateful for getting past certain tribulations while simultaneously incredibly longing for one more chance to see their first smile, to hear the sound of their giggles, or simply the sheer joy of holding your baby in your arms   .... there I go again, tearing up like a big baby myself. The most incredible thing is that these great moments are followed up by their first words, the first time they call you daddy, their first day of preschool, the joy of watching them with their friends, the pure pleasure of cuddling up with them at the end of the day as they get ready to go to bed.

With all these joys comes the responsibility to ensure that every aspect of their wellbeing and nurturing is amply fulfilled with all the love and patience you have plus 1000%. Showing love to your child is the single most important thing right after taking care of all their basic needs. As their parent it is your duty to not only ensure that they are getting the food and clothing they need but also that they are getting the proper nutrition and healthy habits that will stay with them for the rest of their life. I will probably catch some flak for what I'm about to say, but that hasn't stopped me yet. Child obesity is the parent's responsibility not the child's. Ensuring a heathy diet and exercise rests on you and your spouse's shoulders equally. Teaching your child unhealthy and overeating habits can easily lead to long term struggles with weight that could plaque them throughout adulthood. I will not even begin to mention long term health problems that are linked to a poor diet as an adolescent.

Health and wellbeing also includes making sure your kids have the proper attire for the environment. Here comes another rant. My wife has become a mother to far more than just our children. She has spent so much time at my daughters' schools volunteering that many of their classmates know her more than they know many of the teachers. She told me about a time one winter where she noticed many young 4th and 5th graders standing in line to get into school with no gloves or hats in below freezing temperatures. She asked them where their stuff was, they said they didn't have any. She then asked them if they would wear gloves and hats if she brought them some. Almost all of them said they would. Later that night my wife went out and spent less than $30 on winter gloves and hats for these kids. Not only did the kids thank her for bringing them stuff to stay warm they also wore the gear all winter. I tell this story not to point out how wonderful my wife is, although she truly is miraculous beyond words, but rather to point out how some parents do not take the time or effort to care for the basic needs of their children. I get that not every family is as financially fortunate as mine, but I would go without eating before I would allow my children to go out in this world without being taken care of. It's simply intolerable to send your kids off to school without proper attire, without the school supplies they need, or without making sure they have the food they need.

This part is for the dad's out there, taking care of and being there for your children is equally as much your responsibility as it is your wife's. This includes every aspect of their lives', not just the fun stuff. I don't want to come off as being overly harsh on fathers, but I have seen too many instances where the dad has purposely taken a back seat regarding caring for their children. Don't get me wrong, there are certain things that my wife handles far better than I ever possibly could. When these situations arise or for times when your kids only want mom, trust me it will happen, then you should be handling other household or family tasks while she is busy. When my wife and I got married we always agreed that I would go to work, and she would stay home and take care of the kids. When the kids were young this meant that she was on call 24 hours a day, 7 days a week. Not only did she handle the majority of the things during the day but most of the time she was the one who would get up with them throughout the night. For this reason, I made sure to be there for her and the kids when I got home from work. It doesn't really matter how long or trying your day is I can guarantee that her day will have been equally as tiring, if not more so. We always worked together to care for our children and our household. This means changing diapers, giving baths, washing dishes, mopping the floor, doing laundry, wiping runny noses, braiding my daughters' hair, or simply just spending time with them. As my daughters got older and started full day school my wife's 24-7 job didn't really let up. Instead of caring for them all day she was grocery shopping, buying them clothes, driving them around the four corners of the world, volunteering at their school, as well as many other things that kept our house running like a well-oiled machine. Sure, there were many times where she would take time for herself and relax. After 16 years of going non-stop I think she has earned that and a whole lot more. Besides the fact, as soon as the clock strikes three, she's back on duty until the kids are finally tucked in and fast asleep. I equate my wife's devotion to being a parent the same as have two full time jobs. If you worked 70-80 hours a week with an unpredictable schedule and ever-changing tasks you would need a break as well.

All our efforts of working together as a team allowed us to free up more time to spend together doing things as a family. It also meant that we were there for one another when we needed a break. Just as there are long days for me at work where the only thing I can do when I get home is crash on the couch or head straight to bed, my wife has those days as well. The real key to happiness is knowing your spouse well enough to recognize when they need that break and then stepping up so that they can get some much-needed R&R. It may not happen often but, occasionally, you will both have one of those days. The absolute best way to get through that kind of day is to just persevere and work together as best as you can.

It may seem like I have only focused on the most grueling parts of having children thus far. The reality is that most of these things I have talked about as chores and hard work are some of the best times with your kids. There are very few things in this world that compare to that look of unending indescribable joy and love on your child's face when your spending time with them. There is a feeling deep within your soul that can only be understood by those who have experienced it. Besides the miraculous connection between you and your children you will soon find that the relationship with your wife will continue to grow and become even more rewarding.

Children are like little reflections staring back at us in the mirror.

For years I have heard this age old saying but not until I was a parent for several years did I know it to be true. There are only two possible outcomes from this realization, you will either be incredibly proud of what your child has become, or you will be unconsolably horrified by what you have never realized about yourself. However ominous that statement may be, if your child is exhibiting behavior that causes you to cringe with all your being than the chances are the roots of this behavior can be traced back to you or your spouse. Sure, other family members and their friends can have influence, but their parents are by far the most influential people in their early lives. The scariest part about this realization is not only do you need to address the problem with your child, but you also need to take a good look in the mirror and see if one of you is the source of the problem. The sobering reality of this can be exceptionally difficult as changing your own behaviors can be harder than correcting your children's. Raising my children has not only made me a proud father but it has also made me a better person. Their love and absolute unwavering devotion has taught me so much that I am not sure any longer who is raising who.

I knew this would be a tough chapter to write but I don't think I truly imaged how hard it would be. As I sit here in front of the luminescent glow of my thoughts and emotions I am struggling with finding the words that truly express my feeling towards my baby girls and my wife. The more I search for just the right words the more the tears run down my face. I have come to the conclusion that there are no words that can accurately describe the love I have for my family. The bond we have is stronger than any other. The unending love has no parallel. I am not writing this to brag or to say that your family could not share the same. I am writing this to tell you that this kind of family bond is attainable by anyone, all you need to do is pour your entire soul, your entire being, into making it work. I am certain that I don't have all the answers, only God does, but I can honestly tell you that if you follow your heart instead of your desires then God will help you find a way.

Don't forget you're not just Mom and Dad, you were Husband and Wife first, well hopefully, but you get the idea.

No matter how much I know that my daughter's love my wife and I, I also know that one day they will meet a guy who will steal their hearts and they will venture out on their own. I also know that I will need several boxes of tissues on their wedding day. The weird thing is that my daughters' say I never cry, and for the most part they would be right, except when it comes to them. What they may not yet understand is why I will be crying. Sure, I will be sad that they will not be around anytime I want to hug them. I will definitely miss the family dinners and wondrous vacations we have taken together. The smile on their faces will be ever present in my memories. But none of those things will be the real reason I will be balling my eyes out. The real reason will because I will know that they will now have the opportunity to create their very own "Happily ever after". A "Happily ever after" that will most definitely include the grandparents of their children. Although this day is several years away, both my wife and I know that it will come. When it does come my wife and I will be back to what we started as, husband and wife.

Since our daughters were very young my wife and I have always agreed that we needed to work at being both parents and a loving couple. On the surface this may seem like a fairly obvious statement. In reality, this statement is much more complex than you could possibly imagine. Early in our life together we witnessed as several of our older family members broke apart after 15, 20, and even 25 years of marriage. We couldn't help but wonder what had happened between them that after so many years they were ready to call it quits. Does this mean that they never really loved each other in the first place? Could it be that they just stuck with it for the sake of the kids all these years? What could be so bad that they would want to start over after all that time? One common thread that was present in every case was the fact that their kids had grown up and moved on leaving just the two of them. At first this didn't seem to make any sense, after all, they fell in love and got married as just the two of them.

After numerous discussions and observing these implosions from a distance we came to a realization. As all of us grow older we all change in some way or another. Your hopes and dreams change, your likes and dislikes morph, our personalities shift, in essence we grow up. What this means is that who we are when we fell in love and got married is not who we will be in 25 years when our kids leave the nest. This is not a bad thing in itself but, it is a fact. Of course, your personality will change, how couldn't it after navigating everything life throws at you. This however was not the whole realization that we noticed. The real observation was that these couples that had been together so long had grown up as parents to their children instead of as husband and wife. Now don't think for even one millisecond that I am suggesting that having kids will doom your marriage or that in any way is it the fault of their children. The fact of the matter is that if you spend the majority of life raising your children it is very easy to put your relationship with your spouse on the back burner and forget about it. The realization was that as they grew up they didn't keep their bond as husband and wife as a priority in their lives. This of course meant that once the kids were gone they rolled over in bed one morning and they didn't recognize who they were lying next to. Who is this person? I don't know what they like? I don't know what their passionate about? They realize that there is no connection on any level.

If you have been paying attention, you are probably confused as this may seem to be the exact opposite of what I stated in the last chapter. If you need a refresher course, After God, they (your children) are undoubtedly the single most important person in both your lives. I stand by this statement, but the key here is that I said, "both your lives". The fact is that your kids are the most important part of your life together as a married couple. If you are no longer a loving married couple than you are not doing any favors for your kids. As I stated earlier, your kids will learn more from watching you than from what you say. This is also true for how the two of you are as a couple. If your bond as husband and wife is healthy and strong than they will learn the importance of a healthy, truthful, devoted relationship. If you are distant, indifferent, or dishonest with each other than they will learn those behaviors. In a sense, your spouse comes before your kids. This is somewhat difficult to express because in many instances your spouse will have to take a backseat to your children. The difference is that both parents, united as one, will sometimes need to put their children ahead of their spouse. To help clarify, if your child becomes ill it may be necessary to care for them rather than the needs of your spouse. There are many examples where the needs or wants of your children will trump your spouse's. This doesn't mean that your kids come before your spouse. It simply means, that in certain instances it will be necessary for both of you as parents to put the needs of your children ahead of your individual needs and wants.

From day one of your marriage you need to begin the job of figuring out how you are not only going to keep, but in fact grow the bond between the two of you. This does not stop after you have kids, it only gets more complicated. Nobody said life was easy and marriage is no different. However, like all great things in life, the more effort you put into your marriage the more fruitful the reward. I recently just celebrated twenty absolutely remarkable years with my beloved wife. I can tell you without an ounce of doubt in my mind that our bond has grown one hundred plus times what it was when we said our vows to one another. Think about this for just a minute. Picture how incredibly in love two people are on their wedding day. It's supposed to be the happiest day of your life, right? I argue that it should not be the happiest day of your life but rather the happiest day of your life up to that particular point, the best days are yet to come.

Don't ever stop dating your spouse! This may seem like an odd statement, but this is one of the things my wife and I have done to build our bond. This doesn't just mean you both get dressed up and go out to dinner and a movie once a month. This means that both of you need to keep doing the things you did when you were trying to get the other person to notice you. This means you need to flirt, joke around, embrace one another, listen to each other, care for one another, fall over yourself to get the door for her, bake his favorite cake for him on his birthday, bring her breakfast in bed for no particular reason, leave love notes on his windshield, go for walks on the beach, talk about your dreams and your fears, cry together, pray together, diet together, watch the bachelor with her, dance together even if there is no music playing, watch yet another Jason Statham movie with him, vacation together, play games together with your kids, and most of all, plan the rest of your life's together.

Mothers don't forget your oldest child, your husband!

Let me start out by saying that I do not believe it is okay for us guys to act like children, well at least not when we have responsibilities to take care of. The point I want to make is that husbands want to get the mama's attention as well. Bare with me for a bit and I will explain this more clearly. Anybody who has ever had children, or for that matter, anybody who had a mother growing up knows that there is no substitute for the mother-child bond. There are certainly circumstances where mothers have distanced themselves from their children but that is a whole different topic.

The fact is that kids will always ask for their mother first and frankly any mother I know wouldn't want it any other way. This in no way should diminish the importance of the bond between the father and his children. I would argue that both the mother and the father are equally as important to their children's lives. However, the fact that remains is that motherly instinct will almost always trump a father's instinct. Let's face it guys, we love the fact that our wives are more loving, caring, sensitive, and tender than us. These qualities are truthfully some of the reasons we probably fell in love with them in the first place. This may seem like a stereotype and there certainly are exceptions to the rule but all that really does is reverse the roles I am referring to. Children will usually call out to the parent that is more tender and tentative than the other one. At the risk of further offending someone I will continue with my premise that the mother will most often be the parent that fills this role.

I know that in my house, "mom!!!" gets shouted out more times in a day than I can even count. Now that our kids are teenagers my wife is a bit more inclined to wait for them to come find her but when they were younger there was very little that could keep her from rushing to their side. This often means that whenever I wanted her attention it would have to wait. I completely understand why this is the case and I accept this fact with absolutely no contention towards her or my kids. After all, if they weren't calling her name they would be screaming for me. I feel that I need to pause here for a second as I am dangerously dangling off the edge of a cliff. I certainly don't believe that my wife should be taking care of our children more than myself, nor do I condone using this fact as an excuse to weasel out of helping your wife out. As I have stated numerous times, part of showing love for your spouse is by doing your fair share for the kids and around the house. The reality of the situation is that often my kids want their mother's help or attention over mine. This may be in part due to the fact that I have two girls rather than boys, but I would argue this would probably not change much if they were boys. Once again, I don't believe even for a minute that this is due to a stronger relationship with their mother than with me, it's just different.

At first you might think that I am saying the needs of my children are always more important than the needs I have as her husband. This in fact couldn't be further from the truth. It's more a matter of timing than it is importance. As a good husband to my wife and a loving father to my children, it is my responsibility to come to terms with the reality that what I want will have to wait, not forever but at least for a little while. This is where I get back to the heading of this topic. As the mother of the household everybody wants her attention, her children, and her husband. I get it, this can be exhausting, especially with younger children. For this reason, I am a firm believer that as a husband and a father I need to understand this and accept the fact that I need to have patience. As I usually do, this is where I flip the table the other way. As a mother you would not ignore one child and give attention only to the others. Therefore, I say that your husband is your oldest child, not just because he acts like one at times, but rather because to you his actions and requests can seem just as demanding as those from your kids. Even though I truly believe husbands need to be patient and understanding of this, it is also not fair or healthy for their wants and need to take a permanent backseat to your attention. The reality of it is that the two of you got married to spend your lives together, not just so that you could have kids and push each other aside.

Many people may think that the guys should just grow up and get over this. However, let me paint a picture for you that might explain this point further. For a moment let's assume the roles were reversed and your children demanded their father's attention more than their mother's. At first, you're probably thinking, "about time, now I can focus on me for a change". This would probably seem like heaven on earth, at least for a while. Eventually you would begin to feel alone, neglected, and unimportant. The biggest problem with both these scenarios is that one of you is left feeling neglected which will most certainly lead to harsh feelings somewhere down the road. What is important to take away from this discussion is the fact that both of you need to be aware of what is happening. You also need to work together to make sure things don't get away from the both of you.

At the center of this, of course, is good communication. I have had to remind my wife several times that it was my turn to get attention. After I am done stomping my feet and throwing a tantrum she comes to the realization that I was feeling neglected. Obviously, I am exaggerating here but I hope that it exemplifies my point. It is very important that the two of you work together to not only manage her sanity with the kids but also to ensure that both of you get the attention from one another that you crave. If the two of you didn't get married with the intent of spending more time together than you didn't pay attention to the first few chapters of this book.

It is very easy to fall into this sort of situation as, at first, both of you will be overwhelmed with everything that comes with being a new parent. Don't let things continue like this for too long though. Remember what I said earlier about how we change as we get older. That means while one of you is feeling neglected both of you are changing and you could begin growing apart rather than stronger together.

Family is important to raising your kids,
not only for them but also for your relationship.

"It takes a village to raise a child." This proverb bears a lot of truth and it should not be dismissed. The fact is that your children learn, and copy, from all the people they spend any significant time with, including those who you may not be aware of. This means that your children grow up not only based on your values and teachings but also those of the people you trust your children to spend time with. It is also true that they learn and mimic those that you would rather they have nothing to do with, such as certain friends, celebrities, sports superstars, etc. You can't control every person your child meets or admires. However, both you and your child will most likely be better off if you have a say in who they spend most of their time with. This is where family should play an important role in raising your children.

Over the years my wife and I have been blessed to be surrounded by our family and friends. To be honest this has not been entirely just good luck but rather a conscious choice. A choice, that at times, may seem more complicated than a blessing but a choice nonetheless. Many people think it is easier to run away or distance themselves from family when things are not going their way. During times of disagreement or anger this may in fact seem like the only option. However, there are several good reasons why this is almost never a good idea. Of course, there are a few exceptions where distance may be the only answer, but this is a topic for later.

Your family should be the most dependable support structure that you can rely on. You and your spouse grew up with them and you should know them better than most everybody except for your spouse. Keep in mind I said that you know them. I didn't say that you necessarily agreed with them or that they are the perfect role model for your children, but at least you know what you're getting. I may make jokes about this but for most people your family serves as a major support structure for you, your spouse, and your children. A support structure that you can trust, that is faithful to you, and that would go to ends of the Earth to keep your kids safe. I know that not everyone is as fortunate as my wife and I and this is rather disappointing. Families break up, family members make bad decisions, or they take the wrong path. For the most part I would like to believe that these situations make up the minority of the cases, but I also am not blind to what goes on around me. This is one of the reasons why I include close friends as part of your family. Sure, they're not from the same DNA but neither is your spouse, or at least I hope not. My wife and I have several lifelong friends that I would trust with my life, others I wouldn't trust with a pet fish. Both cases may also be true for some family members as well. The important thing is to know which family and friends will always stay true to you and then do all that you can to keep them close, both figuratively and literally.

I know so many people that have moved away from friends and family only to regret that later. In some cases, the distance may be no more than 30 or 40 miles but even this can make a big difference. For the last twenty some years I have worked 30 miles or more away from our home. We chose to not move closer to my work for the sole purpose of staying closer to our families, our friends, and our church. It made more sense for me to commute 30-45 minutes each way to work than it would have to ask our families to drive that distance on a regular basis. The fact is that our life was made simpler and more rewarding by having several friends and family members within 10- 15 minutes of us. It made getting a baby sitter for date night a no brainer. We could easily drop the kids off while my wife and I ran errands. Someone was always just down the road if the kids got sick or needed to be picked up at school. Aside from the long list of conveniences that result from having your support structure close by the list of other benefits far outweighs anything else. Being able to drop by any one of their houses at a moment's notice just makes for a happier and healthier lifestyle for you, your spouse, and your kids.

My daughter's still drop by their grandma's house just to say hi. Their older cousins drop by our house almost daily just to visit. My daughters decide to spend the night at their Aunt's house at the last minute just because they need a change of scenery or because they want to spend time with their younger cousins. My brother drops in just to talk or to show me the cool new gadget he just got. Family get togethers happen more frequently than if everybody had to drive an hour to get there. As I said this list is endless and I will spare you the trouble of reading through dozens of examples that all lead to one thing. My daughters have grown up knowing the importance of family and most of all they have grown up and learned things my wife and could not have taught if it was just us raising them. In addition, my wife and I have been able to take the needed break when we wanted to spend time with just the two of us.

Aside from family there will also be a plethora of other individuals that your children will interact with. What this means for you as parents is that you should truly know and approve of those people that are interacting with your children. This attentiveness should start when they are born, and it ends when you die. Well... not really when you die...but although your influence will fade as they get older, you should be keeping a keen eye on who they associate with for the foreseeable future. The watchful oversight truly ends when they have proven they can pick the right people to surround themselves with, this most certainly includes their future spouse. I know this may seem like I am an overprotective parent and that my kids must hate me for budding into their business. After all what teenager wants their parents looking over their shoulder and telling them who they should be friends with, or God forbid, who they should date. To the contrary this couldn't be further from the truth. If you do it **right** and **explain** to your kids from a very young age why you do everything you do, then you have a good chance that they will welcome your input throughout their life. It is also very easy to go too far with this approach. You may be in the clear prohibiting your 8-year-old from hanging out with certain friends you don't approve of, this however will most likely not succeed with your teenager. When I say to handle this in the **right** way I am referring the absolute necessity to clearly convey your reasoning for this action to your child. "Because I said so" or "because I'm the parent" may keep them away from that trouble maker when they are young, but you will have set yourself up for failure later in their life. Take the time to sit down with your child, on their level, and have a real conversation with them. I also do mean that you literally should sit down so that you are talking to them face to face. Bringing yourself down to your child's eye level is a nonverbal communication that indicates you are taking the time to truly listen to them. Having a discussion with your child will let them know your listening to them which goes a long way. You may still be forced to put your foot down in the end, but the extra effort will make a difference down the road when they are older. Their needs to be a balance here as full detailed dissertation will not be well received or even understood. Keep in mind that at any given point your child is probably only hearing half of what you're saying, if you lucky it will be half. Following this practice with my daughters proved to have an amazing outcome. In most cases we didn't even need to explain to them why they should disassociate with certain individuals. They came to many of these decisions on their own based on prior discussions we had with them through the years.

.

Chapter 8

Caution… teen years ahead … hang on parents, it's going to get a little bumpy.

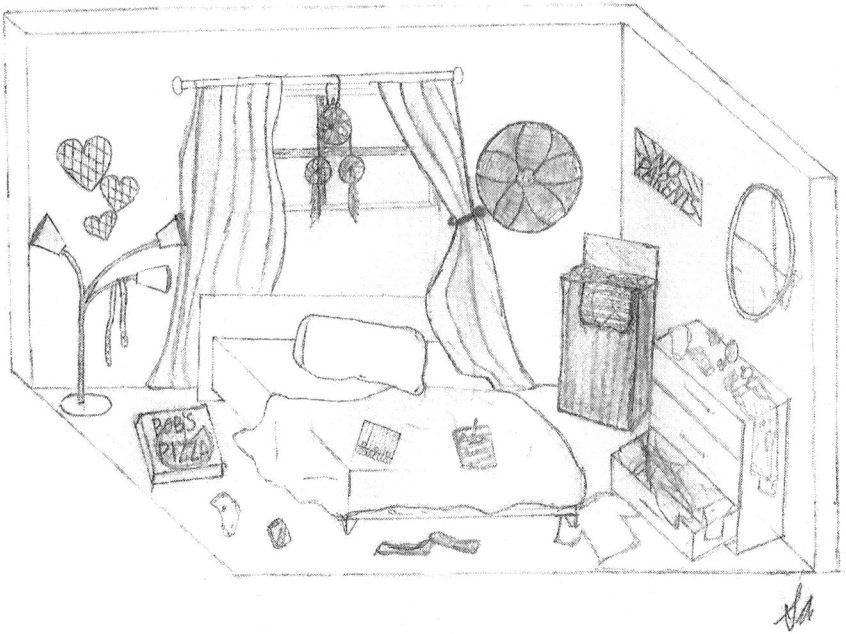

So, you have just spent the last 13 years of your life tending to every aspect of your son or daughters needs and desires and now they are old enough to start taking the reins. Wrong!!! I am sorry for anybody who may have gotten their hopes up after the opening sentence. Even though your children can now care for their basic needs like getting dressed, taking baths, and feeding themselves the teenage years bring a whole new set of challenges for them, and for you. This means it is time for a pivot from what being a parent has been defined as over the past decade or more. You have had to help them with their school work and guide them through the occasional mishap with their friends or the playground bully. You have dealt with some defiance of your rules, struggled with getting them to do their choirs, and labored over getting them to keep their room from looking like a scene from 'The Walking Dead'. All of this will seem like mere child's play when you meet your new adversary.... Hormones!!! I'm not just referring to the physical changes that come with puberty but the very real and highly unpredictable emotional roller coaster you are about to unwilling board.

Now that I have thoroughly scared and horrified you I will also tell you that both you and your children will survive the next 5 years. You will also find that the first 13 years of loving and caring for your children will bring rewards that you have never dreamed of. Every morning when I wake up I thank God for giving me the chance to see what wonderful young adults my children have grown into. Each day brings another entirely different reason for me to be proud of my daughters. From their many accomplishments at school to how they pass love and tenderness to their grandparents, their cousins, their family, and their friends simply amazes me. I know that I have made mistakes as a father but you sure couldn't tell from looking at my daughters. They have become strong, independent, intelligent, courageous, and loving young ladies. There are no words to describe the lengths I would go to ensure the safety and happiness of both my daughters and my wife.

You might be asking how I went from **doomsday** to **utopia** in only two paragraphs. The answer is simple…"no pain, no gain" (Jane Fonda, 1982), "without risk, there is no reward" (R. Mayer, 2008), "the best things in life come to those who work for it" (Anonymous).   As I have said before, relationships are hard work. This is true for both parenting and marriage as well as friendships. If you approach each of these relationships with love in your heart and God by your side, you will be wealthy beyond belief. A wealth that money cannot buy no matter how much you have.

13 is the new 3

No, I haven't lost my mind, at least I don't think so. I was once told by my brother-in-law that you can describe teenage behavior by subtracting ten years from their age. At first, I didn't really understand what he meant but soon enough it was abundantly clear. As your child's eyes begin to open to the great big world in front of them they tend to challenge the status quo. Much like when your 3 or 4-year-old may have decided to test the boundaries of your rules they tend to repeat this behavior between the ages of 12 to 14 or 15. Obviously these ages are merely indications as every child is unique with their own free will. It will also seem like some of the good habits that you've worked so hard to instill in your child will now mysteriously disappear as if Will Smith erased it from their memory. All those years of getting your kids to clean up after themselves might have been better spent trying to solve world hunger. There have been times where my wife and I have just thrown our hands in the air and said, "I know we taught them better".

The good news is that just like the years of dissent when they were younger this phase will only last a few short years. The key is that both you and your spouse need to uphold a united front and stand your ground. Under no circumstances should you allow your children to bully either of you into getting their way. One important thing to remember here is that your kids are getting older and developing their personalities and character. The last thing you want to deal with as a parent of a teenager is your child pushing back on your kingdom that you have worked so hard to build. But, you also want to teach your children to be strong leaders and for them to stand up for what they believe in. Now is the time where you will need to pivot your parenting style from an oligarchy to something closer to a democracy. As the parents you still have the final say in the matter, but you need to seriously listen to their concerns and compromise wherever you can. Another age old saying, "pick your battles carefully." This wisdom is very applicable in this area. If you try to win every disagreement with your child, you will inevitably wind up losing the war. Eventually your child will rebel against your rulings and you run the risk of losing your relationship with them for several years if not forever.

Explain your decisions at every point in your child's life.

One of the very important rules of child rearing is to always remember throughout their entire life is to always explain the reasons for your decisions. Explaining yourself to a 6month old is a bit ridiculous, but from a very early age you should always explain why you're asking them to do something rather than just proclaiming "because I said so". Explaining to a toddler that the stove is hot and that you don't want them to get hurt makes perfect sense. This is no different than explaining to your teenager why they can't go to an unsupervised party. Granted the conversation will be much more involved but explaining to them what could go wrong and what your concerns are will pay off in the long haul. A parent who repeatedly just says no and then sends them to their room becomes a "mean parent". A parent who explains the reason they said no may still be considered a "mean parent" but the latter shows your child that you truly care for their wellbeing. It also shows them that you have considered their feelings. This distinction is very important because, whether your teenager will admit it at the time or not, what they really want is your love and care. For this to be effective you will most certainly need to learn the importance of compromise. If your child feels that you never give into their requests, they will stop listening to your reasons because from their viewpoint you're not listening to them either.

It should be no surprise that there are many similarities between your relationship with your spouse and your relationship with your children. The fact is that you are raising your children with the intent of them becoming young adults. If you don't start treating them as young adults how will they ever learn to become one. Just as a lioness teaches her cub to hunt it is your responsibility as a parent to teach your children how to be a strong, confident, intelligent, and passionate adult. It is these traits among others that will ultimately make them successful in both their professional and personal lives.

Your kids are unique individuals, don't compare your kids to one another, or anybody else for that matter.

Under no circumstances should you ever use one of your children's behaviors, good or bad, as an example of how another should act. This will never be seen as fair treatment by your kids. I have seen all too often where one child is trying to live up to the expectations of their parents while in the shadow of their sibling. Despite our best efforts my daughters have mentioned this to us on more than one occasion. Every person on this planet is unique with their own interests, desires, strengths, weaknesses, and talents. Your children are no exception to this. It is your responsibility as their parent to recognize each of these aspects that define their unique personalities. You may have one child that excels at sports while the other excels at academics. No matter what talents or weaknesses they possess, you have one mission as their parent. Your goal is to congratulate them on their accolades, push them to improve upon their weaknesses, and to help them discover who they are as an individual. I cannot stress enough the importance of your role as a parent. God has entrusted you and your spouse with **a life, your child**, where your sole responsibility is to protect them from harm and to raise them in God's image. If you're not up for such a monumental responsibility…. well then… too late… your already in the chapter on teenagers so there is no turning back now… buck up and get over it…your children and God are depending on you.

You may want to pause here for a moment to catch your breath as I did just drop that bomb on you out of nowhere. I make jokes to keep this book from becoming too dry and uninteresting, but this point is very serious. I do not take being a parent lightly and I really do not have much patience for parents who are "phoning it in" or doing enough to "just get by". I know that despite my best effort I will still make mistakes and that there will always be things I could have handled better. This is all okay, but be certain of one thing, the day I stop trying to improve is the day I have failed God, my wife, and most importantly my children.

The biggest concern that you face with your teenagers is losing their respect and trust.

This may seem completely backwards at first, after all, they're the teenagers who show no respect and do things of questionable integrity, right? The reality is that by the time they are showing you disrespect and doing things behind your back you have already lost their trust. Remember, kids learn more from watching what you do than what you say. You can't expect them to live up to rules that you do not adhere to yourself. Telling them to do one thing while you do the opposite not only sends mixed messages, but it also tells your kids that your rules only apply to them. This may be the case for some things like bedtime and perhaps finances but everything else is pretty much fair game. Let's go back to the example of your child putting his or her hand on a hot stove. You wouldn't tell them no and then turn around and put your hand on a hot burner. The same is true for so many other things in your life. You can't expect your teenager to refrain from swearing while you cuss at them because they didn't do their choirs. If you're telling them to do their homework, then you better be sure they see you doing yours. By yours, I mean you sitting down with them to help. Yes, this is part of the job of being a parent. The same goes for choirs, housework should be divided up among all household members. Expecting your children to do all the work is called "child labor", not parenting. Chore sharing should start much earlier than the teenage years but it's never too late to teach good work ethic.

If you don't want your kids to lie to you then don't show them it's okay by lying to them. The truth may be harder to explain but it is a lot easier than having to rebuild trust between you and them. If you lie to them so that they do what you want, they will only learn that this behavior is acceptable for them to get what they want. Lies will always come back to haunt you regardless of how small or how good intentioned they may have been. Even lying about the family gold fish swimming away to a better place is only an attempt to delay the reality of life. I know that this means you will have to have some difficult conversations with your kids but shielding them from reality by lying to them is only setting the both of you up for issues later. We will leave Santa, the Easter Bunny, and the Tooth Fairy out of this. They are all real.... nudge...nudge. Just like childhood stories they are intended to spark imagination and inspiration and I do not classify them the same as what we are discussing now. I know that sometimes it may seem better to spare them from the harshness that reality can throw at us from time to time. However, being honest with your kids will help them when they must face the same situations head on later in their life. It will also help them to keep their trust with you.

It is very important that your teenager knows they can come to you with anything, no matter how bad it may seem. This is very important towards keeping trust with your child. If you tell them they can come to you with anything then both you and your spouse need to make sure you hold up your end of that deal. This means that you're not allowed to yell at them or ground them without discussing what happened. I am not saying that bad behavior should go unpunished but how you handle the situation will dictate how future mishaps are handled by your child. If you handle it badly than you stand a very good chance of losing their trust and the next time they make a mistake they may decide not to come to you with it. If you handle the encounter with calmness and fairness than you have a good chance of further cementing the trust between you.

I would be lying if I told you that I was always able to remain calm when my kids came to me with these types of things. Sometimes it may be necessary for everybody to go to their corners, a.k.a. "bedrooms", while everybody calms down enough to discuss the situation. The seize fire time should however be several minutes to a couple hours rather than several hours or even days later. It is very important to come back together in a relatively short period of time to calmly discuss things. I can't emphasize enough the word **discuss** in this context. If you make this a one-sided lecture you may win the fight, but you will most likely lose the war in the long run. Having a true discussion means that you and your spouse truly listen to what your child has to say. Truly listening means NOT cutting them off mid-sentence. It means trying to put yourself in their shoes for the moment. It means you may have to bite your tongue for the time being. Depending on the situation, this may require a Herculean amount of restraint on your part. So much so that you may even wind up in the running for the Nobel peace prize. The calmer you are and the more you listen to their side of the story the more you will gain their respect. With your respect they will also be much more likely to respect and honor whatever punishment you and your spouse decide.

The punishment should fit the crime. Grounding them for three months because they forgot to turn in their homework may not only be obsessive, but it may also have the opposite effect. Part of respect and trust comes from dealing with someone in a rational, fair, and compassionate way. Let's put it this way, you wouldn't find it fair if your boss suspended your pay for three weeks if you were 15 minutes late to work for the first time. If you show up late consistently over an extended period, your boss would be justified in docking your pay or issuing a warning regarding your employment status. The same holds true for your kids. Coming home 15 minutes late from curfew should probably be met with a warning the first time. The second and third time with a few weeks needs to be met with stronger restrictions like grounding or loss of privileges. It is also very important that both you and your spouse agree on the punishment and that both of you adhere to the consensus. Not doing so teaches your child a very bad lesson and it will most likely lead to complications between you and your spouse. This is not to say that the punishment can't be reduced or revised based upon good behavior or further consideration. It is however important to ensure that your child understands the relevance and importance of your rules. The punishment also needs to be consistent among your children. There are few things that will chip away at your child's trust and respect faster than biased or unfair treatment among siblings. Age certainly serves as good justification for slightly varying punishments and rules, but this must also be explained to all.

Despite what kids say they thrive on rules and structure.

It was both refreshing and rather odd for my wife and I to hear from our daughter's friends that they wish their parents had instilled more rules in their own homes. Very few people in this world are comfortable with constant change in their lives. People generally feel more at ease when they know what to expect. In life there are very few certainties and at times it can seem overwhelming when you don't know what's around the corner. If you take a moment to think about this from your child's perspective it might seem even more unrelenting. From the time they were born your kids are introduced to new experiences nearly every day of their lives. They are constantly meeting new people and they are expected to learn new things each day of their lives. For some kids this never-ending onslaught of change is exciting, and it will feed their inspiration. However, as stated earlier, most us are creatures of habit and most of us like stability and routine. Your child is no exception to this rule. It doesn't matter if they are 3 or 13 years of age, stability and routines help children to feel safe, relaxed, and loved.

It may come as a bit of a surprise or a bit odd that I am making the connection between structure and love. In fact, you might hear from your teenager that you don't love them because you won't let them do what they want. This couldn't be further from the truth. Let me explain using a few examples. When you first bring your new baby home from the hospital you and your spouse are responsible for every aspect of your child's life. Food, warmth, safety, comfort, and health are just a few of the items on a very long list of responsibilities as a new parent. As parents we do these things because we love our children and we want them to be happy and safe. At this young age it is easy to see how your child is fully reliant upon you. What bothers me the most is that some parents think these responsibilities completely transfer over to their children as they get older. It's very true that as they get older they will be able to feed, dress, and bath on their own. It is expected, and extremely important, that your children learn the responsibility of caring for themselves. However, as a loving and caring mother or father it is your responsibility to still show your love by making sure they not only do these things but that they learn the right way to care and provide for themselves. As I have said before, child obesity is the fault of the parents not the child. This is also true for their manners, their choice of clothing, their sleep habits, their interactions with other people, and basically every aspect of their daily life. Being a parent is the most important, toughest, and rewarding job you'll ever have. There is no other profession or career in the world where you have the sole responsibility of molding the life of another human being. Your responsibility as a parent does not end when your child is 18 or even 21. Your love for your children should transcend time and age.

Sure, you're not going to be able to show your love in the same ways as your children get older. While bathing your 3-year-old is great, doing the same for your 15-year-old is, well... not okay. Making sure they eat breakfast and wear a coat when it's minus 15 outside does show your love while also teaching them good habits and making sure their safe. Trust me, your kids will not always think of this as love at the time, apparently when you become a teenager you also become impervious to subzero temperatures and a coat is no longer required...or so they think. Loving your child is NOT letting them leave the house wearing less clothing than a Victoria's Secret model just because it's the new fad or because it's "lit", apparently this is the new word for "cool". I get the fact that that your child will not turn to you and say, "thanks Mom or Dad for telling my outfit is inappropriate, I will go change into something more suitable". Loving your child is standing your ground and enforcing your rules. Not by yelling but by leading by example and by explaining why you want them to change. Sure, it is easier to let them go without the struggle and letting them figure it out for themselves. If you do, they may figure it out on their own but trust me when I say that 10 years or even 2 years down the road your child will turn around and thank you for enforcing your rules. It is much easier to enforce these rules if you have been doing so since they were young but even then, it may be very difficult. It is also never too late to instill good behaviors and habits in your children.

As with everything in life, balance of rules and structure with freedoms is absolutely crucial. The polar opposite of a parent who enforces no rules or structure for their children is one who is overbearing and restrictive. This parenting approach may be effective at first, but it can and often does result in the opposite behavior from your children. Rules that are too strict or too demanding can lead to many issues with your children. It is important to protect your children from the bad things in this world but if you never let them venture out into the world they will never be ready to leave the nest. Worse yet, your child may become so enraged with your strict ways that they will revolt and head in the wrong direction. You might be asking yourself, "so how do I know what the right balance is". The scary answer is you will never know the perfect balance. You will make mistakes and there is no single answer that fits all children or all situations. All you can hope for is that you get close enough to the right balance for your child. This should result in them seeing the love you have for them and ultimately staying within the bounds that you set. The only way to ensure success is to involve your child in the process. In this respect the relationship with your child should mirror that of the relationship with your spouse. It's all about communication and compromise. The main difference is that as the parents you get the final say and your kids should know this. If you have the right conversations with them, you will rarely need to drop the hammer and enforce martial law. Part of finding the right balance will most certainly include a few times every so often where you need to reevaluate your decisions and rules and admit to your child that you were wrong. Like I said, you will make mistakes just as your child will. If you can't admit you were wrong to your children, then don't expect them to admit they were wrong to you.

The Hardest part about being a parent is coming to the realization that if you did your job right ...your children won't need you anymore.

The sign of a great leader (or parent for that matter) is when the people you were leading no longer need to follow you. It's not a sign of failure but rather a sign of success. A true leader builds up the ones around them and then basks quietly in the shadow of their accomplishments.

As a parent and as a professional this is one of the greatest lessons I have ever learned. Nothing makes me prouder of my daughters than sitting back and watching them take the lead. They both leave me beaming with pride and love the way they have learned to lead and mentor others. The best part about it is that they also understand the sheer magnitude of the statement above. It feels great to be the leader, but it feels indescribably amazing to know that your part of the reason someone else has become a great leader. Anybody can be a follower, some people think their leading only to find out later that nobody's following them, but truly great leaders didn't ask to lead... their followers appointed them the role. This doesn't happen by chance however. In order to lead others, you need to be able to demonstrate leadership while also inspiring others to participate.

I also want to point out that it's okay to be a follower sometimes as well. The fact is that if everyone was in a leadership position than there would be nobody left to follow the leaders. A leader with no followers is alone, not a leader. This may seem obvious but there is a very important point behind this. There are two very insightful phrases that accompany this school of thought.

"Lead, follow, or get out of the way", (Thomas Paine)

This first statement is very clear. If you're NOT, the designated leader than get out of the way of progress and find the right person to follow. This is in no way an indication that you should teach your kids to blindly follow a leader. The point is that if a person believes in the values of the leader and that leader believes in what they are doing than the rest of us should get out the way. Quick checkup here, this of course does not apply to ungodly, immoral, or reckless behavior by the leader or the group.

"If you want to go fast, go alone, if you want to go far, go together" (African Proverb)

Some circumstances require quick decisive actions. For these circumstances you, and your children, may find it more fruitful to go it alone or as part of a small team. You'll never win the race if you wait for the person pulling up the rear of the pack. However, if your climbing a mountain you may need that person moving steadily along at the back to make it to the top. They might be trailing in the back because their carrying all the supplies. These analogies are just a few examples of how each situation can be different depending on the goal and the circumstances.

It is important to teach your children when it's best to follow, when it is a good time to take the lead, and when they should just step aside. For those old schoolers, "you've got to know when to hold'em, know when to fold'em, know when to walk away, and know when to run." (Kenny Rogers, 1978)

Chapter 9

We've hit a rough patch; how do we fix it?

For starters, the key word in title of this chapter is **we**. Marriage is all about compromise and communication. If things don't always turn out the way you want in a relationship it may be due to the way you're looking at the problem. There is also a fifty-fifty chance that you're the problem, or at least part of it.

The path to fixing your marriage should start with a hard look in the mirror

It seems to go against human nature for us to admit when we are wrong and even harder for us to recognize when we are the one causing the issue. In practice, looking inward at a situation is the first place you should start. Each one of us was created in God's image but, let's be truthful, we are not perfect by any chance. We all have issues that we need to work on and the first step is identifying the problem followed closely by admitting this to both our spouses and ourselves. Causing undue drama in a marriage to later find out that you were the one that was wrong is a big mistake. I want to stress that this does not mean that you should adapt if the problem truly lies with your spouse. However, in my experience most issues in a marriage are in fact two sided. The fault may not be equal between them but in many cases neither person is 100% error free. This of course is not an absolute as I have seen several instances where the fault was most certainly entirely the fault of one person.

If you still feel that the error in fact rests solely on the shoulders of your spouse, it doesn't mean you can expect them to fix it all by themselves. The fact is, if they knew how to fix the problem then they most likely would not have caused the problem in the first place. You might even find they are completely oblivious to the issue altogether. Which is another problem on two fronts. First, they are either not very good at listening to you or they could care less. Second, if you haven't communicated the issue to them then the issue partly lies with you. I mean **communicate** in the verbal sense of the word, with words and conversation. Subtle hints, brooding, and hidden messages don't count has communication in this instance. Subtle hints and hidden messages are great for expressing love for one another, but they are not sufficient when conveying discontent. If your spouse is not listening to you or if they seem to simply not care than this is certainly the sign of a much bigger issue. This will especially be the case if they will not reveal to you why they are acting this way. In both cases you may in fact need help moving forward.

In some situations, you may need outside help to figure out what the real problem is. There is no shame in this. Marriage counseling is a very good option when you're trying to fix your relationship. This can be from a professional or from your pastor, but it probably should not be a friend or family member. Family and friends are great support during times of need, but it is nearly impossible for them to remain impartial in the situation. Family and friends will tend to lean towards where their greatest loyalty lies. Marriage counseling of course does require both spouses to be willing though. Dragging your spouse to counseling may not be effective if they are unwilling. Convincing an unwilling spouse to go to counseling can prove to be a challenge. This may especially be the case if you are placing all or most of the blame on them. This may be an instance where taking some of the blame upfront will help convince them to go. I am not suggesting that you lie to your spouse only to trap them into going. What I am suggesting is that you take a step back and even for just a moment consider that your spouse's rebuttal arguments are based on reality. I know to some people this may be very difficult as I am asking you to "take an L". The better way to view this is not as losing the argument but rather view it as a substantial effort towards not losing the war. After all, if your marriage ends in separation or divorce than neither of you will feel like you came out a winner.

There are no winners when a relationship or marriage breaks apart. Even if you were undisputedly not in the wrong, you will still come out of the matter with harsh feelings and at least a small amount of remorse and emptiness.

Divorce is not the reset button people think it is.

From my perspective divorce is not an option. However, divorce is sometimes the only viable outcome. These two statements seem to completely contradict each other but let me explain. Let's put this in a different context that may help make my point. Pretend for a moment that you are traveling down a dusty country road in your car. All of a sudden, from out of know where, a giant seven-foot-tall moose steps into the middle of the road and you don't have enough time to stop. To your left is a corn field but you can't see what's beyond it, to your right is a small ditch and some brush. Which option do you pick? The corn field may seem safe but what lies beyond the unknown, a boulder, a fence, a tractor, it's impossible to tell? The soft ditch will be bumpy and will certainly damage your car, but you pretty much know you'll come out okay? Regardless of which option you chose, you probably didn't even think of just continuing straight head on into the moose. That's because when a car hits a moose, nobody wins, you or the moose. Essentially, continuing the same path was not even an option you would consider because it would most certainly end in death or at least severe injury. Now I will probably catch flack for killing a moose in this story but stay with me. This story is meant to be a similarity for marital issues. If you continue on the path your relationship is currently heading, then your marriage will most likely end in divorce and someone is going to get emotionally hurt. Choosing to act and do something about it offers no guarantee of success but it's certainly better than the alternative.

Divorce can't always be avoided as sometimes it's simply not up to you. If your spouse decides to leave you despite your best efforts this is not your fault and not your decision. The important thing is to know that you truly tried. This of course means exhausting all your options and putting effort forth as though your life depends on it. In extreme cases involving mental, physical, or sexual abuse there is no question, divorce is the only viable outcome. Under no circumstances should a spouse or their children be subject to these horrific acts. A person who knowingly and willingly inflicts physical or mental harm towards their spouse or their children is beyond the reach of reason and understanding. Drug and alcohol abuse do not excuse or explain this behavior. If you or anyone you know is a victim of abuse, please seek protection and remove yourself and your children from harm's way. A list of resources is provided in the appendix of this book.

Cheaters never prosper

Lack of faithfulness to one another is obviously one of the biggest transgressions that can tear apart a marriage. However, adultery does not necessarily signify the end of your marriage. I know it's easier to sit here and scribble words onto a page rather than living through it but bear with me for a moment. Once again, there is no excuse or a "get out of jail free card" for this betrayal of trust. Cheating is undeniably just as bad if not worse than lying to your spouse. Both are a huge violation of trust and both actions will be very difficult for the other spouse to "forgive and forget". I can tell you that no matter how difficult it can be to regain that trust, it is possible. There are very few marriages that survive adultery but those that do are a sign of a very strong and loving spouse. If you are the one who committed adultery and your spouse is willing to work through it, I strongly suggest you bend over backwards to make it work. The odds are slim to none that you will find another person as brave, indescribably strong, and incredibly loving as them in your lifetime.

Even though I can't speak from direct experience on this topic, I can offer insight based on what I feel has worked for strong people around me who have endured the unthinkable. The only way your marriage will work long term is if you truly learn to forgive the indiscretions of your spouse. This certainly will not happen overnight and in fact it will most likely take several years to put things back together. An absolute is that you will gradually have to forgive what happened as your spouse works to slowly rebuild your trust. If you force your spouse to live under your thumb or require that they perpetually "walk on ice" than there is a real possibility they will eventually give up trying and leave, or worse yet, decide to cheat again. I am not suggesting that either of those actions would be justified but nobody wants to live the rest of their life wearing a scarlet letter. It will undoubtedly also keep the two of you from getting closer as your spouse will most likely not feel like an equal.

For the offending spouse you must agree to absolute transparency in all that you do. Where you go and who you talk to must not only be forthcoming but also be unsolicited information sharing with your spouse per their discretion. It's up to you to earn their trust once again. It is not up to them to grant you trust you have not worked to earn. It will be a long road to recovery but if you truly put in the effort it will pay off in the end. For whatever reason you decided to cheat it is up to you to make sure those circumstances do not arise again. Whether it was a bad decision while you were drunk or a conscience decision because you felt like something was missing, it is your responsibility to avoid or fix those circumstances going forward. If you felt something was missing from your relationship than it is your responsibility to discuss with your spouse and to come to a compromise on a mutually agreed upon solution. If it was a compromising situation with a coworker or an ex than it is up to you to avoid putting yourself in those circumstances in the future. If it's because you can't remember due to a drunken stupor than you need to get help as you are most likely an alcoholic. Whatever the reason or the excuse it is not justifiable. It was an error and you must own it, don't blame others for your decisions. It might seem like I am being heartless and unforgiving, conversely, I am being stern and supportive. People make errors, those who own up to them and make amends with those they have hurt are truly worthy of forgiveness. This is not only my belief but the way of God.

Chapter 10

Empty nest, who's this person in bed next to me? 18 or more years of marriage while raising children will change both of you.

I considered leaving this chapter to a later update of the book since as for now I cannot speak to this with firsthand experience. I decided to touch on this topic briefly based on the observations I have seen from friends and family close to us. I still believe my advice here will be sound. Much of what I have talked about in this book is based upon implementing behavior observed from people around us.

This is also a good point to talk about my methodology for charting the course ahead. Relationships are a lot like the engineering principles I have learned throughout my career.

- The future is uncertain and only careful thought and experimentation can help chart the way.

- Tread carefully and concisely, as with relationships, electronics will blow up in your face if you make the wrong mistake.

- Failure is not only an option, it's an absolute certainty. It is rare to get it perfect, or even on par, the first try. The key is to learn from your mistakes and try a new approach the next time.

- Hard work and determination will pay off in glorious dividends.

- Learn from what others did before you, both successes and failures.

- Make sure what you're working towards something that others want to be a part of. Otherwise you wind up with a gizmo you can't sell or worse yet, a personality nobody wants to be around.

- Patience and perseverance are essential to reach success.

- Communication is the most important part of any project, especially relationships.

- Remember to have fun and take time to play. Tesla was a brilliant man and his contributions to science have shaped much of the world today, but he also died a crazy lonely man.

- Under no circumstances ever, touch a high voltage circuit with a grounded scope probe, this one may only pertain to engineering but it's good advice regardless.... trust me!!!!

- If something can go wrong it probably will, plan accordingly and be prepared to make changes as you go.

- The devil is in the details, always make sure you find the root of the issue or it will come back and bite you in the a**.

- Logical thinking will get you the best results most of the time but sometimes you must just go for it and follow your gut.

- Don't let the fear of failure stop you from pursuing greatness. Failure is another word for learning.

- Be sure to listen to others around you, I promise you that you're not always the smartest person the room. Just ask Aaron Burr.

- Listen to ideas and criticism from both your friends and your foes equally. Just because you don't see eye to eye with another person doesn't mean their wrong. A truly remarkable person listens to all input and then makes a decision that will provide the best outcome.

- Surround yourself with people that you can trust that also challenge you to do better.

- Don't let people who say, "it's impossible" stop those of us who are "making it happen". (Anonymous)

- "No" just means you asked the wrong question. Re-evaluate your situation and your proposal until the only possible answer is "yes". This may mean it was a bad idea or you just failed to make your case effectively. Figuring this out can be tricky but understanding why you were told "No" will most likely lead you to formulate a proposal that is far superior.

- No good decisions are made after 2am, get some sleep and start fresh the next day. If you work the night shift, just add 12hours to this. The main point here is not to make critical decisions when you're not performing at peak mental capacity.

The interesting part about this chapter is that so much of the advice and principles I have talked about in the first nine chapters serve as a prerequisite for success at this point in your life. A great relationship is like a building, if not built on a solid foundation it will crumble around you no matter what you do. It's not to say that there is no hope for you If you don't have the fundamentals firmly affixed at your base, but you certainly have some work to do. If your relationship is not built based on selflessness, communication, trust, companionship, and friendship it is not too late to work on what aspect(s) are lacking.

What might surprise some people is that these principles become even more important at this point in your life than when you were both younger and had children in the home. Raising children takes a lot of effort and time. My wife and I have observed on more than one occasion that parenting can wear on your relationship. This is especially the case if both of you are not paying attention to this as time goes by. Before anybody gets outraged about me saying children can destroy your marriage let me clarify what I mean. As I have stated previously, raising children is the most amazing and rewarding experience that you will ever have on this planet. I have also mentioned that it is the hardest and most important job you will ever have. With both of those statements being 100% truthful it should be no surprise that raising children has also distracted the two of you from just focusing on your relationship with your spouse. If it didn't than you weren't paying attention to the entire middle section of this book. However, now that your children have moved out of the nest that distraction will certainly be less than it has been for the past 20 years or so. This will leave a lot more time for the two of you to focus on each other once again as you did at the beginning of your relationship. If fact you may even find a lot more time to be with one another if retirement follows an empty nest.

To better help get my point across I figured I would play out a ridiculous scenario but if you stay with me I promise it will help to clarify. Say for example that you and your spouse are young, you've just met and fallen in love. You spend your days and nights thinking about each other all leading up to your miraculous wedding day. The two of you spend the next few years working on your careers and spending the rest of the time as an inseparable couple. Then out of the blue you have a stranger move in with you that can't do anything for themselves. This stranger requires both of you to provide constant effort to care for them. About the time this stranger starts to be able to care for themselves a second stranger moves in with the same inability to care for themselves. You and your spouse now spend even more time and effort caring for these two strangers. All this time and effort means you have less time to do the things together that you did when you first got married. These strangers stay in your house for the next 18 to 22 years. Meanwhile, these strangers get better at caring for themselves, but they always seem to be around asking for this or that. Then as abruptly as they entered your home they begin to leave, first one than the other. Suddenly when you come home at the end of the day your house is quiet and the only other person around is your spouse.

Now after 20 plus years of caring for these strangers you and your spouse find yourselves alone together. Do you both have the same likes and dislikes? What are you going to do with all your free time? Who is this person in bed next to me? Do I really know them? Do I love them? Do I even like them?

I am sure that most of you figured out the "strangers" in my story represent your children, for the rest of you…look a squirrel. This ridiculous scenario is much closer to reality than most people would want to admit. The fact is that all the distractions brought about for the 20 plus years will without doubt have reduced the amount of time with your spouse. As the two of you grow older, your likes and dislikes will change. Therefore, I have stressed the great importance of making time throughout your lives together to find time for just the two of you. Date nights and "no children" vacations are just a small part of this effort. I truly believe that all the little moments my wife and I spend just the two of us are priceless. Even just embracing each other for a few minutes is like a quick charge for our relationship.

As we get closer to the point where my daughters venture out to start a life of their own I often think about what it will be like when it's just the two of us again. Don't get me wrong, I am in no hurry for my daughters to grow up and the sheer thought of my oldest graduating high school this year brings tears to my eyes every time. Yep, there I go once again. However, I look forward to the time my wife and I spend together. My greatest desire is that my daughters find husbands that they can share the same kind of pure joy with.

I have struggled for some time with how I wanted to end this book. What insights could I provide that my daughters would be able to draw inspiration from? What profound summation could I make that would resonate with others?

I came to the realization that I can't put an ending on something that is just beginning!!!

This may be the end of this book, but it is only the beginning of the rest of my life with the love of my life. It is only the beginning of the wonderful lives that my daughters have ahead of them. The story of my grandchildren is still a distant fantasy. I can't write the next chapter of my life before it's even here.

To be continued...

Appendix

Domestic Abuse Help

As I have stated several times throughout the course of this book, there is no excuse for verbal, physical, or sexual abuse of any kind. If at any point in your relationship you experience these acts please seek help. The situation will rarely improve without external support and in no way does anyone deserve to be treated in such a manner. Aside from reaching out to family, friends, or your pastor, I have included the contact information for The National Domestic Violence Hotline below.

Phone: 1-800-799-7233
Online: www.thehotline.org
Both are available 24/7/365

Alcohol and Drug Abuse Help

Addiction to Drugs and alcohol is both damaging to yourself and your relationships. If you or someone you know is struggling with an addiction, please seek help. I have included a few contacts below.

National Helpline
Phone: 1-800-662-HELP (4357)
Online: www.samhsa.gov/find-help/national-helpline
Both are available 24/7/365

Made in the USA
Las Vegas, NV
25 February 2021

18573576R10087